LIGHTHOUSES SERIES

ENDANGERED LIGHTHOUSES

Stories and Images of America's Disappearing Lighthouses

TIM HARRISON AND RAY JONES

The Globe Pequot Press

Guilford, Connecticut

ABOUT THE AUTHORS

RAY JONES is a writer and publishing consultant living in Pebble Beach, California. He is the text author of Globe Pequot's *American Lighthouses* and all eight books in the colorful Globe Pequot Lighthouses Series as well as the co-author of *Lost Lighthouses* and *Legendary Lighthouses,* the companion to the popular PBS series. Ray has also served as an editor for Time-Life Books, as founding editor of *Albuquerque Living* magazine, as a senior editor and writing coach at *Southern Living* magazine, and as founding president and publisher of Country Roads Press.

TIM HARRISON is the publisher and editor of *Lighthouse Digest* magazine, co-author of *Lighthouses of Maine and New Hampshire* and of the popular children's story coloring book, *The Littlest Lighthouse;* co-founder and partner of Lighthouse Depot in Wells, Maine, which bills itself as "The World's Largest Lighthouse Gift and Collectibles Store"; and co-founder of the Lighthouse Depot Lighthouse Museum, also in Wells, Maine. He is president of the American Lighthouse Foundation, a nonprofit organization dedicated to preserving America's lighthouse history and heritage, and has been active in the restoration of a number of American and Canadian lighthouses as well as the restoration of the gravesites of former lighthouse keepers. Promoting the preservation of lighthouses, he has appeared on numerous radio and television shows, including PBS TV's six-hour miniseries *Legendary Lighthouses* and ABC TV's *Nightline.* He has accumulated an extensive collection of historical lighthouse photographs, many of which appear in this book.

Copyright © 2001 by Timothy Harrison and Ray Jones

Cover and page design by Nancy Freeborn
Cover photograph of Sand Island Lighthouse near Mobile, Alabama, by Bruce Roberts

Library of Congress Cataloging-in-Publication Data

Harrison, Tim.
  Endangered lighthouses : stories and images of America's disappearing lighthouses /
Tim Harrison and Ray Jones.—1st ed.
    p. cm.
  Includes index.
  ISBN 0–7627–0815–8
    1. Lighthouses—Conservation and restoration—United States.   I. Jones, Ray, 1948–   II. Title.

VK1023 .H3697 2000
387.1'55'0973—dc21

                                                                                    00–057673

Printed in Canada
First Edition/First Printing

CONTENTS

Michigan's Crisp Point Lighthouse shows off a fresh coat of paint. For now the light is safe from the encroaching Lake Superior shoreline, but there is still much more work to be done.

LIGHTHOUSES ON THE EDGE

*M*any of America's most important and beloved monuments are in danger. Every day the weather chips away at their crumbling brick, stone, and mortar. Dry rot gnaws at their supporting wooden beams. Vandals deface their walls and smash their windows. Floodwaters undercut their foundations, threatening to bring them crashing down into a formless jumble of broken walls and shattered lumber. Unless something is done to protect them—and soon—they will be lost forever.

Nothing speaks more eloquently of a people than the structures they choose to preserve and cherish. Consider the pyramids of Egypt, the Taj Mahal of India, or the Eiffel Tower in Paris. Each of them is a profound symbol, a powerful, revealing statement on the meaning of civilization. It is hard to imagine our world without them.

In Washington, D.C., the Jefferson Memorial, Lincoln Memorial, and Washington Monument celebrate the beliefs and aspirations we share as a nation. The loss of any one of these historic edifices would be unthinkable. And yet we are on the point of losing dozens—if not hundreds—of our historic lighthouses, all in their own way important monuments much like their more famous cousins on the Mall.

Lighthouses rank among the oldest buildings in America. They are historical treasure houses with much to teach us about the engineering marvels of an earlier era, the outward-looking attitudes of our forefathers, and the personal sacrifices made by keepers in the name of humanity. Because these towers were built and because of the men, women, and even children who kept their beacons shining, countless ships, cargoes, and passengers reached their destinations safely. Countless lives were saved.

American leaders recognized the importance of lighthouses early on. One of the very first acts of Congress created the Lighthouse Service, an agency that served America proudly for nearly 150 years. Most of the lighthouses we still see today were once staffed by Lighthouse Service personnel, but in 1939 the U.S. Coast Guard took responsibility for all our navigational aids, including lighthouses, and the old Lighthouse Service ceased to exist.

By the middle of the twentieth century, modern technology had begun to make lighthouses less necessary for safe navigation. To save money, the Coast Guard boarded up one lighthouse after another, removing their full-time keepers and replacing their priceless glass Fresnel lenses with plastic optics operated by remote control or by automatic timing devices. Since the primary missions of the Coast Guard were law enforcement and search and rescue, the agency had little or no time and money to spend on the preservation of historic structures.

As a result, many unused lighthouses were destroyed or sold at public auction, often at very low prices. Fortunately a chorus of public protest eventually put an end to that wanton and destructive policy. Nowadays the Coast Guard does its best to preserve what lighthouses it can, but lacks the funding to maintain them all. Some have been given to the National Park Service, while others have been handed over to state agencies, local communities, and nonprofit historical foundations. For many other old lighthouses, unfortunately, there have been no takers, forcing the Coast Guard to board up the windows and abandon them.

Of the more than 1,600 light towers that once marked our nation's Atlantic, Gulf, Pacific, and Great Lakes shores, fewer than half remain. Of those that have survived, more than a few are now in dire straits, some on the very point of collapse. But in every coastal region and state dedicated preservationists are fighting to save them.

This book is dedicated to America's endangered lighthouses and to all those now working hard to restore and preserve them. The following sections tell a few of the happier preservation success stories. After that, we'll take you on a nationwide tour to visit some of our less fortunate coastal treasures—the forgotten lights, the doomsday lights, the lights that may very well be about to disappear.

A SWAN ON THE POTOMAC

Just on the other side of the Potomac River from the great white monuments of the nation's capital stands a small whitewashed wooden building. Though less imposing than the marble giants across the river, it is nonetheless a monument of national importance. Its stature is so modest that it could easily be taken for a country schoolhouse or even a tenant farmer's shack, but in fact it once played a vital role in the life and economy of the entire Potomac region. It is the Jones Point Lighthouse.

During the nineteenth century, the Chesapeake and Ohio Canal linked the farms, sawmills, and mines of the Appalachians to the navigable waters of the Chesapeake Bay. A steady stream of mule-powered barges flowed down from the mountains, bringing coal, lumber, and produce to the port of Alexandria, Virginia. Seeking loads of these valuable bulk commodities, oceangoing freighters reached Alexandria from the bay via the winding Potomac. To guide them into port around the last snaking bend in the river, in 1856 the government established a navigational light on Virginia's Jones Point.

A rather humble facility by almost any standard, the Jones Point Light Station consisted of a simple one-and-a-half-story wood-frame building with a tiny lantern set atop its pitched roof. Completed for less than $5,000, including the cost of land, lamps, glass, and fittings, it surely ranks among the least expensive lighthouses ever built. Just as surely, it was one of the government's all time best-buy bargains. The little light station survived flood, fire, rot, and civil war while serving mariners faithfully for seven long decades. Amortized over the seventy-year active life of the station, the lighthouse had cost taxpayers about 20 cents a day.

The Jones Point Lighthouse as (left) a near complete ruin following World War II, and (right) a partially restored monument.

In 1924 a disastrous flood wrecked the C&O Canal. By that time commerce on the antiquated canal had already slowed to a trickle, so the canal was never rebuilt. Shipping traffic on the Potomac had petered out as well, so in 1926 the Lighthouse Service extinguished the Jones Point beacon.

Because of its historical significance, the little lighthouse was given to the Mount Vernon Chapter of the Daughters of the American Revolution. The gift turned out to be an ugly duckling—the term "white elephant" hardly seems to fit in this case. The DAR could afford only limited upkeep for the building, which seemed in constant need of paint and roofing.

With the outbreak of World War II, the U.S. Army took control of Jones Point, and the lighthouse was all but destroyed as a result. Loitering soldiers gutted the building, sometimes even using it for target practice. By the time the DAR recovered title to the property in 1953, the lighthouse could only be described as a ruin. For decades it languished in disuse and disrepair. Boarded up to keep out vandals, it received an occasional coat of paint, but not much else in the way of maintenance. But timely assistance from the National Park Service saved it from further damage and perhaps utter destruction.

Today the lighthouse is part of a fifty acre Alexandria city park including biking trails, a soccer field, and picnic areas. Those who visit the park during the day may not realize the little wooden building is a lighthouse, but at night its true character shines through. Relit in a 1993 ceremony that brought tears to the eyes of many DAR members, the Jones Point beacon once again sparkles in the waters of the Potomac. Erosion and vandalism, however, remain serious threats to the structure, which has never been completely restored. The last chapter of the story of the Jones Point Lighthouse remains to be written.

A GIANT TAKES A WALK ON THE BEACH

Half a world away from America's Alexandria an ancient city by the same name once announced itself to mariners with the boldest beacon and tallest light tower of all time. For more than a thousand years the harbor of Alexandria, Egypt, was marked by the Pharos, a giant limestone tower believed to have soared 400 feet or more into the Mediterranean sky. So impressive was the Pharos that the ancient Greeks included it—along with another lighthouse, the Colossus of Rhodes—among their seven wonders of the world. The Pharos might still be standing had it not been thrown down by an earthquake during the Middle Ages.

America has its own giant lighthouses too. And there are many who consider them wonders. Perhaps the most famous of them is the brick titan that marks Cape Hatteras on the North Carolina Outer Banks. The huge Cape Hatteras tower with its black-and-white barber-pole stripes is as familiar to Americans as the Statue of Liberty, the Golden Gate Bridge, or almost any other man-made structure that one can bring to mind. That's been true at least since 1999, when the Hatteras Lighthouse became headline news across America and throughout the world. In June and July of that year, the 130-year-old tower made the front pages of newspapers throughout the country as well as the six o'clock news on every television network. The reason: This extraordinarily historic structure was in serious danger, and a bold plan had been put into action to save it.

The current Cape Hatteras Lighthouse is the descendant of an earlier tower built in 1803 on orders of President Thomas Jefferson. The 95-foot brick sentinel, later raised to a height of 150 feet, marked one of the most dangerous coastlines on the planet. The storm-swept

Outer Banks beaches and the treacherous Diamond Shoals that lie just off the cape had claimed thousands of ships, along with their hapless passengers and crews, and had earned a grim reputation as the "Graveyard of the Atlantic." Mariners needed all the help they could get to safely navigate these turbulent waters.

The original Hatteras tower served for nearly seven decades, during which time a parade of history passed within sight of its light. Slave ships and China clippers, cotton freighters and Civil War gunboats moved up and down this coast. Some never made it past the shoals.

Still warm from its famous duel with the Confederate ironclad *Virginia*, the turreted Union warship *Monitor* went down in a gale near Diamond Shoals while being towed south for blockade duty. Following the war federal authorities decided Cape Hatteras needed a taller tower that could do a better job of warning ships away from the shoals.

Completed in 1870, the new 200-foot-tall Cape Hatteras Lighthouse was then one of the loftiest structures in America, if not the world. Its powerful first-order Fresnel lens projected a beam that could be seen from ships more than 20 miles at sea. And the tower was made to last. It was a behemoth—with walls several feet thick containing more than a quarter million hard-baked bricks. It must have seemed to the island laborers who built the tower brick by brick for $1.50 a day—not bad pay at the time—that their handiwork would stand forever. Indeed, the massive building would survive hundreds of gales and hurricanes and may yet survive hundreds more. But nothing can resist the destructive force of the ocean itself.

When the last course of brick was laid on the tower in 1870, it's not likely that anyone gave much thought to erosion. At that time the tower was located a full 1,500 feet—more than a quarter mile—from the ocean waves. As the years went by, however, the Atlantic moved closer and closer. The sea level has been creeping upward since the end of the last Ice Age some 10,000 years ago, and this has caused sandy barrier islands such as the Outer Banks to migrate toward the mainland. By the mid-1990s the inexorable westward march of the Atlantic had brought its waves to within a few dozen yards of the tower's foundation. Some feared the big lighthouse would come tumbling down in the next hurricane.

Over the years government engineers had fought back against the rampaging Hatteras beach erosion with dikes, breakwaters, revetments, sandbags, concrete and steel groins, and a beach replenishment program involving literally millions of cubic yards of sand. But nothing worked for long. As the close of the millennium approached, it became clear that the ocean waters would soon claim the Cape Hatteras Lighthouse. In a last-ditch effort to save the nation's best-known land- and seamark, the National Park Service—now in charge of the building—hatched a daring plan to move it to a new site more than half a mile to the southwest

With Atlantic waves threatening the historic Cape Hatteras Lighthouse (above), a special roadway (left) was built so the tower could be pushed back from the water and out of danger.

Engineers (above) prepare to move the giant tower (right) recognized throughout America as a national treasure.

and well away from the rapidly eroding beach.

The plan stirred up a storm of controversy. Some believed that moving the lighthouse would destroy its historical significance. Others maintained that the 2,800-ton structure was simply too big and too fragile to be moved safely. Underlying these arguments were fears on the part of local landowners that, after the move, the government would cease its beach replenishment efforts, thus placing their beachfront properties at risk. In the end, despite a war chest of more than $1 million—much of it kicked in by land developers—the effort to block the move failed.

Spurred on by the approach of the annual hurricane season, the National Park Service launched the relocation effort in June of 1999. The engineering and mechanics of this complex operation were placed in the competent hands of the International Chimney Company of Buffalo, New York, and Expert House Movers, a Virginia company. Both firms were veterans of previous, seemingly impossible lighthouse relocations, such as those at Rhode Island's Block Island Southeast Light Station (1993) and the Cape Cod Light Station in Massachusetts (1996).

On June 13 the enormous tower was lifted by a precisely balanced bank of hydraulic jacks and lowered onto a series of roll beams. Four days later, shortly after three in the afternoon, the tower was carefully shifted 4 inches to the southwest. Thus began the amazing journey that would carry the Cape Hatteras Lighthouse to the safety of its new home some 2,900 feet away.

The tower traveled much faster in the days to come—an average of just over 100 feet a day. Even so, it took almost four weeks for the lighthouse to reach its destination. Crowds of up to 20,000 bystanders gathered to watch its progress. What they saw was hardly scintillating. The tower's motion was barely perceptible, but most thought the spectacle inspiring nonetheless. So, too, did national television audiences who were treated to regular news reports on the tower's progress. Then, to the accompaniment of sirens, horns, and an entire country breathing a collective sigh of relief, early on the afternoon of July 8, the tower was pushed the last few feet onto its new platform.

The much publicized plight of the Cape Hatteras Lighthouse and its successful relocation has focused fresh attention on our national heritage and the need to preserve historic structures. Perhaps for that reason, lighthouses are more popular now than ever.

LAST STAND ON MOHEGAN BLUFF

Among the most astounding lighthouse rescues ever conducted was that of the handsome Victorian tower and residence located atop Mohegan Bluff on Rhode Island's Block Island. Seriously threatened by erosion, this classic New England structure could only be saved by moving it back from the edge of the cliff. This was no simple task.

Constructed during the mid-1870s at a cost of $80,000, the Block Island Southeast Lighthouse consisted of a 67-foot octagonal brick tower attached to a rather elaborate duplex keeper's residence. The building appeared far too delicate to be moved. However, a special team assembled by International Chimney Company and Expert House Movers—the same two companies that would later handle the Cape Hatteras move—solved the technical problems. In August 1993 the lighthouse was hoisted onto rollers and pushed back several hundred feet and out of harm's way.

A dedicated preservationist group called the Block Island Southeast Lighthouse Foundation managed to raise about $2 million in private and federal funds to pay the cost. Thanks to their efforts, the fine old lighthouse will not share the fate of the Mohegan Indian war party that made an ill-fated raid on Block Island in 1590. Defeated by local island warriors, the raiders made their last stand on the heights now known as Mohegan Bluff. Rather than surrender, the Mohegans leaped over the cliff to their deaths.

A proud Victorian empress, the Block Island Southeast Lighthouse has been rescued from the threat of erosion.

AN OLD NEW ENGLANDER TAKES A STEP BACK

Few lighthouse success stories are as notable as that of the famed Cape Cod Light in Truro, Massachusetts. Established in 1797 and rebuilt in 1857, it served many generations of New England whalers and other Atlantic mariners. Also known as the Highland Light, the station was located on a formidable 120-foot bluff. Together with the 66-foot tower, the bluff gave the beacon considerable elevation, making it visible from more than two dozen miles at sea. But the bluffs were also a threat. Composed of compressed sand, the Truro heights have steadily crumbled, sometimes at an alarming rate. By the early 1990s, the lighthouse stood near the very edge of the precipice. If something had not been done to protect this extraordinarily historic structure, it might already have collapsed into a jumbled heap at the base of the cliff. But something was done.

Usually the only way to save a coastal structure from erosion is to move it. That was certainly the case with the endangered Cape Cod tower. The erosion could not be stopped, so the tower had to be moved. As one might expect, this was an incredibly difficult and expensive task. The price tag approached $1.5 million, and local preservationists, led by the Truro Historical Society, scrambled to raise the money. In addition to private donations, financial assistance was provided by the National Park Service, the U.S. Coast Guard, the commonwealth of Massachusetts, the town of Truro, and even a nearby golf course.

Pulled back from a crumbling precipice, Cape Cod's famed Highland Lighthouse now stands at the edge of a golf course.

With financing in place, the project got under way in 1996. The extremely difficult and delicate task of moving the 430-ton tower was assigned to a team of experts from the International Chimney Company. First the walls of the 140-year-old tower were protected by a concrete compression ring within and a steel jacket without. Next the foundation was excavated and heavy steel beams inserted beneath the tower. Lifted with hydraulic jacks and mounted on rollers, the entire structure was set onto rails like a huge caboose. Then the tower retreated from the cliffs along the rails at a pace so painstakingly slow that the crowds who came to watch could barely detect the motion. Coins placed on the rails were squashed paper-thin by the slow-moving lighthouse and later auctioned off to pay a tiny part of the cost. The move to safety took eighteen days to complete.

Today the Cape Cod Lighthouse sits beside the seventh fairway of a golf course several hundred feet from the cliffs. Erosion is unlikely to threaten it for at least another hundred years. The tower is, however, occasionally struck by an errant golf ball.

THE IRON SISTER VERSUS
THE NO NAME STORM

Not long after the move of the Highland Lighthouse was completed, the International Chimney Company turned its attention to an equally endangered tower at Nauset Beach near Eastham some 15 miles or so to the south. The bluffs at Nauset Beach were falling away even faster than those at Highland. In October 1991 the so-called No Name Storm washed away huge chunks of the cliff. Within three years more than 30 additional feet of the weakened bluff had vanished, leaving the tower little more than a dozen yards from the precipice. It became obvious that the next big storm might spell doom for the fine old lighthouse.

The cliffs at Nauset Beach had been eroding for a long time and had wreaked havoc on several earlier light towers. Originally three small brick towers stood here. Affectionately known as the "Three Sisters of Nauset," they displayed a highly unusual triple light, which mariners could easily distinguish from the twin lights then shining at nearby Chatham and Plymouth. Built by Winslow Lewis in 1838, the three towers served until the 1890s, when the advancing erosion forced construction of a new set of sisters located further from the cliffs. Eventually these towers were threatened as well, and in 1923 they were replaced by a single tower moved here from Chatham.

A brick-lined, cast-iron tower some 48 feet in height, the relocated tower stood well back from the cliffs, far enough to protect it from erosion for the better part of the twentieth century. But by 1996 the lighthouse was running out of real estate.

To save it, movers lifted the ninety-ton tower and pulled it to a new site more than 300 feet away. In all the project cost $330,000. A federal grant provided much of the money, and the rest came from private contributions collected by the Nauset Light Preservation Society. Decommissioned by the Coast Guard in 1993, the beacon has been relit as a private aid to navigation.

Lighthouse Digest by Bill Quinn

This view dramatically illustrates the plight of the Nauset tower before it was relocated during the 1990s.

POUNDING NAILS AT RACE POINT

Lighthouse stories abound on Cape Cod. Among them is that of the Race Point Lighthouse near Provincetown, about 10 miles northeast of Truro. Established in 1816, the light station here marked a stretch of turbulent and treacherous currents generated by the inward curling sands of the Cape. Over the better part of two centuries, the Race Point Lighthouse helped mariners navigate these dangerous waters. Even so, more than a few vessels wrecked on the sandy beaches of the point.

Until just a few years ago, the Race Point Lighthouse was itself a wreck. The isolated sta-

tion was never popular with keepers, who found the loneliness of the place hard to endure. The light was automated in 1978 and the two-story wooden residence boarded up. After automation the often harsh Cape Cod weather began to take its toll on the buildings. The brick-lined cast-iron tower became streaked with rust, and the dwelling fell into disrepair.

"This is the one that was forgotten, the one everybody walked away from," says Jim Walker, chairman of the Cape Cod Chapter of The American Lighthouse Foundation.

Located well away from the touristy center of Provincetown, the station might have been abandoned altogether if not for a group of local lighthouse enthusiasts. In 1995 the foundation leased the property from the government, and before long Walker and other chapter volunteers set to pounding nails and painting. Mostly they used their own tools and donated materials. Over time the leaky roof of the keeper's residence was repaired, the chimney rebuilt, and the interior restored to livable condition. Equipped with space heaters, flush toilets, refrigerator, stove, and hot running water, the dwelling is now open to guests for overnight stays. Once a year, in October, the foundation offers the residence for an artists' residency program.

The dilapidated Race Point Lighthouse (left) and residence (right), have been painstakingly restored, and now serve as a handsome reminder (above) of Cape Cod's maritime past.

9

A MERIT BADGE FOR ST. HELENA

The New England Lighthouse Foundation is not the only high-quality volunteer organization that works hard to preserve old light towers. In the Midwest the Great Lakes Lighthouse Keepers Association is the best friend of lighthouses in need. Among their most notable projects is the ongoing restoration of St. Helena Island Lighthouse in Lake Michigan.

Built in 1871, the St. Helena Lighthouse guided ships headed for the strategic Mackinac Straits linking Lakes Michigan and Huron. After the station was automated in 1922, the 71-foot brick tower and attached dwelling suffered greatly from neglect and vandalism. It might have fallen into ruin. However, the Great Lakes Lighthouse Keepers Association believed it deserved a better fate and shouldered the formidable task of repairing and caring for the structure. As with many of its other projects, the association has involved other organizations in the work at St. Helena Island. For several years Michigan Boy Scouts have earned Eagle Scout badges by helping with restoration work.

(Above) The St. Helena Light during its active years.
(Left) Today the tower is being restored with the aid of Michigan Boy Scouts.

Wayne Sapulski

U.S. Coast Guard

NEW HOPE AT CRISP POINT

It seems incredible that the Crisp Point Lighthouse has not been forgotten altogether. The light station here was closed up in 1930, almost a lifetime ago, and no one has found any practical use for it since. For one thing, the old, orphaned lighthouse is located far off the beaten path. You won't pass the abandoned tower on the way to anywhere else. To reach it you must drive westward from remote Whitefish Point on the Michigan Upper Peninsula and follow a sandy, single-lane road for 14 miles through a dense hardwood forest. The last part of the journey is made on foot through grassy lake dunes.

When you finally arrive at the tower, you may wonder how it has survived, more or less on its own, for all these years. Mighty Lake Superior has pushed back the shoreline and seems about to pull the tower down into its chilled waters. No doubt the lighthouse would be lying in the lake today had it not been for some timely assistance from unexpected quarters.

Established in 1904, the station was given a two-story, brick keeper's residence, a 58-foot brick tower, and a fourth-order Fresnel lens, which displayed a red light. It was assigned the task of guiding ships along the Upper Peninsula lakeshore and, more important, of warning them away from the deadly shoals that lay just off Crisp Point.

Because it was so difficult to reach and supply this remote outpost, the Lighthouse Service closed the residence in 1930 and automated the light. Since that time the facility has received little maintenance. The residence and other buildings were demolished in 1965 to discourage vandals, and the tower was left more or less on its own.

The chief threat to the tower is Lake Superior itself. The storm-driven waters of the lake, which once stood more than 700 feet away, have washed away the shoreline until, by the 1990s, the lake stood at the very foot of the tower.

At this point a pair of dedicated preservationists, Don and Nellie Ross, entered the picture. The couple stumbled across the faded tower while tramping through the Upper Peninsula back country during a 1988 vacation. Afterward they were haunted by images of the failing lighthouse, and in time they decided to make a retirement project of its rescue. In 1996 the Rosses moved to the little town of Paradise, Michigan, some miles east of the lighthouse, and founded an organization called the Crisp Point Lighthouse Historical Society.

At first the Rosses believed their restoration efforts would consist primarily of patching walls, repairing the roof, and slapping on a fresh coat of paint. As it turned out, however, saving the lighthouse proved far more complicated than they had imagined. Late in 1996 Lake Superior swallowed up the entrance to Crisp Point Light tower. Next it

Ryan Ross

The troubled Crisp Point Lighthouse.

Great Lakes Shipwreck Historical Society

The Crisp Point Station with keeper's residence during its active years.

Morgan Curry

Lighthouse Digest

*Photographs document the destruction
after storm-blown waves crushed the
entrance to the Crisp Point Light tower.
Dedicated restoration efforts have since
repaired some of the damage (see page iv).*

Nellie Ross

would probably take the tower itself—and sooner rather than later.

As a stopgap measure to hold back the lake, the Rosses organized the placement of three-ton sandbags around the base of the tower. But the only permanent solution would be a rock breakwater. To build it, nearly fifty loads of stone had to be hauled from a local quarry and dumped into the lake along a 600-foot section of shore in front of the lighthouse. This would cost up to $42,000. Fortunately the contractor agreed to haul the stone first and let the money roll in later. Thanks to donations by many generous people and organizations, including the American Lighthouse Foundation and two local Indian tribes, the necessary funds were raised.

For the moment, at least, the Crisp Point Lighthouse is safe, but much more work needs to be done. Like many lighthouses it remains endangered, but with friends like Don and Nellie Ross, this old Lake Superior sentinel is more fortunate than most.

Read on and you'll learn about dozens of other endangered American lighthouses.

ENDANGERED TOWERS OF THE EAST

Nova Scotia to the Chesapeake

Endangered Towers of the East

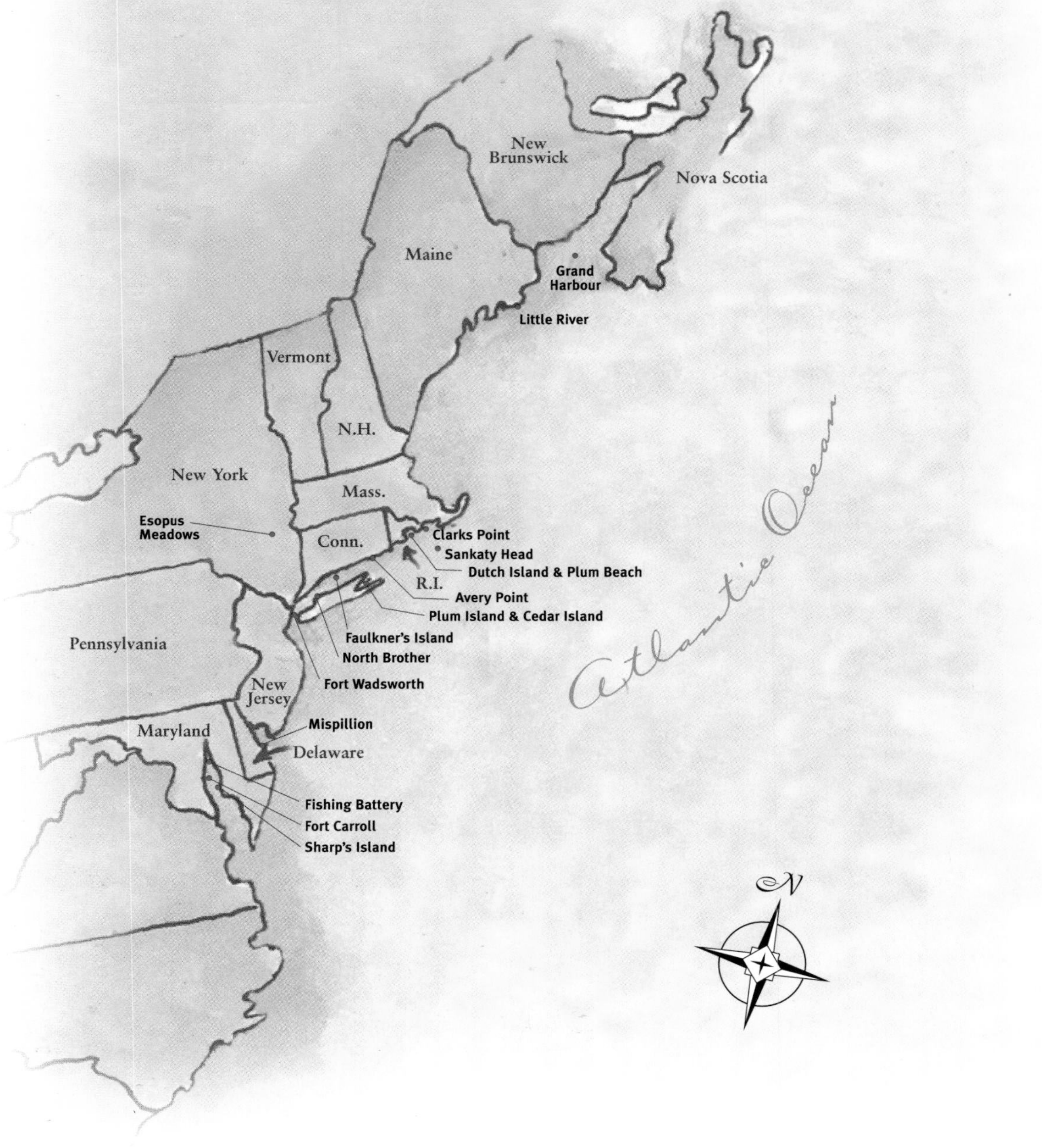

New Brunswick

Nova Scotia

Maine

Grand Harbour

Little River

Vermont

N.H.

New York

Mass.

Esopus Meadows

Conn.

Clarks Point

Sankaty Head

Dutch Island & Plum Beach

R.I.

Avery Point

Plum Island & Cedar Island

Faulkner's Island

North Brother

Fort Wadsworth

Pennsylvania

New Jersey

Maryland

Mispillion

Delaware

Fishing Battery

Fort Carroll

Sharp's Island

Atlantic Ocean

N

GRAND HARBOUR LIGHTHOUSE

Grand Harbour, Nova Scotia

1879

Canada's Grand Harbour Lighthouse on Ross Island in Nova Scotia has been described as North America's most endangered lighthouse. Indeed, the 120-year-old wooden residence and tower may have a date with doom. Its walls are a shambles, and the entire building sags perilously toward the waters of the fabled Bay of Fundy. The troubled lighthouse, however, is not without its friends. Preservationists in both Canada and the United States are fighting to save it.

The plight of the lighthouse has nothing to do with the quality of its construction. It was the work of George and Charles Short, master shipwrights who took great pride in their work. The Short broth-ers completed the project on a thrifty budget of $1,050 Canadian, and the station's light was first displayed in 1879. Afterward its beacon guided vessels in and out of the harbor for more than eighty years. The light was finally snuffed out and the station abandoned by the Canadian Coast Guard in 1963.

Unfortunately little maintenance has been done here since the last keepers departed in the 1960s. Left to stand alone against wind, wave, and storm for more than thirty years, the orphaned building has begun to fall apart. Recently money has been raised to shore up the lighthouse and save it from collapse, but at least $60,000 will be needed for a complete restoration—nearly sixty times what it cost to build the lighthouse in the first place.

Grand Manan Maritime Museum

Lighthouse Digest

This vintage photograph shows the Grand Harbour Light Station during its active years. The people seated beneath the walls are likely the keeper and his family.

Much of the historic Grand Harbour Lighthouse now lies in a jumble. At least $60,000 is needed to restore it completely.

LITTLE RIVER LIGHTHOUSE

Cutler, Maine

1847 AND 1876

Of the many scenic structures clinging to the rocky coast of Maine, few are as long on history and—until recently—short on friends as the Little River Lighthouse. In 1847 Congress appropriated funds for a light station to be built on the east side of Little River Island, not far from the down east village of Cutler. After having guided vessels in and out of the Cutler harbor for almost 130 years, the station was shut by the Coast Guard in 1975 and its light moved to a nearby iron skeleton tower. Afterward the old lighthouse fell onto hard times. Of little use to the government and unwanted by others, it became a sort of orphan.

In 1993 the Coast Guard offered the historic 35-foot iron cylinder tower, detached clapboard dwelling, oil house, and boathouse to the town of Cutler, which declined ownership.

Five years later the Little River Lighthouse became one of more than twenty Maine lighthouses put up for "adoption" under a special statewide program. Even though it was now officially listed on the National Register of Historic Places, no one wanted this particular foundling. Declared excess property by the government, it seemed likely to be destroyed by sheer neglect. The story of the Little River Lighthouse may yet have a happy ending, however. The American Lighthouse Foundation recently took charge of the station and is raising money to restore its buildings to their original condition.

U.S. Coast Guard

These three photographs show the Little River Station as it evolved over the years. (Top left) The tower and attached residence built in 1847. (Bottom left) The station as it appeared after 1876, when the original tower was torn down and replaced by the existing one. (Below) The station as it appears today.

Timothy Harrison

U.S. Coast Guard

CLARKS POINT LIGHTHOUSE
New Bedford, Massachusetts

1869

round 1800 the town of New Bedford, Massachusetts, sold the federal government a small parcel of land at Clarks Point for use as a light station. By 1804 a 42-foot stone light tower had been built there, and for sixty-five years its light guided fishing boats and freighters in and out of the busy New Bedford harbor. However, the Civil War convinced military officials that the harbor needed to be defended, and a seven-sided granite fort was built on the point during the 1860s. The massive stone walls eventually blocked the Clarks Point beacon, and in 1869 the lantern room was lopped off the old tower and placed on top of the fort. The delicate lens and lighting mechanism in the lantern room were provided with special cushioning to protect them from the concussion of the huge guns

at the fort. As it turned out, this precaution proved unnecessary, since the guns were never fired—in anger or otherwise.

In 1889 a more effective navigational light was placed at Butler Flats near the entrance to the harbor, eliminating the need for the Clarks Point beacon. That same year the tiny lighthouse atop the fort fell dark, and its lamps were never relit. The fort and its lighthouse have stood disused and empty ever since. Both have suffered heavily from time and vandals, who find this spot attractive because of its isolation. Although restoration work was done on the lighthouse during the 1970s, vandals completely reversed its good effects and, in fact, practically destroyed the historic lighthouse.

New Bedford has ambitious plans to restore the tower once again and to rekindle its beacon. The city is already in the process of putting the old fort to use. Its high walls will hide a sewage treatment plant. Plans call for the city to restore the fort and open it as a public park.

In 1869 the Clarks Point lantern was removed and placed atop the walls of an adjacent stone fortress. This is how the station looked before it was discontinued in 1899.

The small, rectangular stone tower of the Clarks Point Lighthouse bears the marks of more than a century of neglect and abuse by vandals. Fortunately it may soon be restored.

SANKATY HEAD LIGHTHOUSE

Nantucket Island, Massachusetts

1850

ime may be running out for one of Nantucket's most visible landmarks. The Atlantic Ocean is gobbling up the high, sandy cliff that separates it from the base of the Sankaty Head Lighthouse. Known to mariners and landlubbers alike for the distinctive broad red band that cuts across its middle, the tower is one of many American lighthouses threatened by erosion. In this case, however, the threat is imminent. The edge of the cliff now lies little more than 100 feet away, and each year the ocean moves a few feet closer. The average annual rate of erosion is 5 feet; as much as 8 feet of the cliff has vanished in a single year.

Little thought was given to erosion when the Sankaty Head Lighthouse was built in 1850 to help mariners negotiate a maze of vaguely charted shoals off Sankaty Head. The tower stood safely back from the sea, and its position atop the high cliff was considered ideal. Boosted by the bluff, the 70-foot tower placed its light at a commanding elevation of more than 150 feet. Shining seaward from such a height, its powerful flashing beacon could be seen from ships more than 20 miles away.

Ironically the station's lofty perch may now prove its undoing. Threatened by the steady retreat of Sankaty Head, the old tower must be moved within the next few years or it will fall over the cliff. When the steadily advancing erosion threatened the Sankaty keepers' dwellings—unoccupied for years—they were moved out of danger and given to the community for use as low-income housing.

Moving the 600-ton tower to safety will not be quite so easy. One plan for saving the structure calls for moving it back several hundred feet to the edge of an adjacent golf course at an estimated cost of $2 million. However, a recently installed erosion control system, consisting of pipes and pumps placed under the sand, seems to have temporarily halted the crumbling of the cliff face. Meanwhile the scenic tower still remains an endangered lighthouse.

This photograph dramatically illustrates Sankaty Head Light's peril. The keeper's dwellings shown here have since been moved away from the eroding cliffs.

Sankaty Light, Siasconset, Nantucket Island, Massachusetts, Built 1850

An antique postcard proudly displays Nantucket's Sankaty Head Lighthouse. Notice the broad red band on the tower.

18

DUTCH ISLAND LIGHTHOUSE
Narragansett Bay, Rhode Island

1826

*L*ong ignored and almost forgotten, the remains of the Dutch Island Lighthouse cling precariously to a scrap of rock about midway along the west passage of Rhode Island's famed Narragansett Bay. Much of the station, including the old two-story, Federal-style dwelling, has already disappeared, and today, only the squared-off tower still stands. The Dutch Island Preservation Society is struggling to preserve what remains of the abandoned structure. The concerned local citizens now have the help of The American Lighthouse Foundation, which has licensed the lighthouse from the U.S. Coast Guard.

The rock-strewn Narragansett was once among the best lit bodies of water in the United States. Among the many sentinels guarding its heavily trafficked shipping channels was the Dutch Island Light Station, established in 1826. The original light tower and keeper's residence were built of slate quarried locally on the eighty-one-acre island. Apparently the workmanship was not of the highest quality, as government inspectors would later call this "the worst built lighthouse in Rhode Island."

Reconstruction work costing about $4,000 was completed in 1857. That same year the station received a fourth-order Fresnel lens, a vast improvement over the Winslow Lewis lamp-and-reflector optic that had served here—and poorly—for more than thirty years.

The refurbished station withstood accidental fires, countless gales, and more than one major hurricane. Seemingly the only disaster the lighthouse could not survive was abandonment. The Coast Guard automated the light in 1947, and to save the cost of maintenance, the fine stone keeper's dwelling was demolished in 1960. In the 1950s the island was turned over to the state of Rhode Island. The Coast Guard kept the beacon shining until 1979, when it was extinguished by vandals.

(Left) Rhode Island's Dutch Island Lighthouse as it appeared early in the twentieth century. Keepers lived year-round in the two-story dwelling beside the tower. (Right) The dwelling was removed more than half a century ago. Today only the square tower remains. The American Lighthouse Foundation is raising funds to prevent further deterioration and restore the tower.

PLUM BEACH LIGHTHOUSE
Jamestown, Rhode Island

1869

Every day thousands of motorists crossing Rhode Island's Jamestown Bridge are treated to a view of the Plum Beach Lighthouse rising from the blue waters of Narragansett Bay. The lighthouse is rather pudgy in appearance, resembling a big coffee pot or—a more frequently made comparison—a spark plug. In contrast the bridge itself is long, sleek, and modern in style. Even so, the two structures have a lot more in common than one might think. Both were constructed primarily of concrete and steel, and both, in their own time, served as navigational aids, marking the bay's heavily trafficked channels and helping countless travelers reach their destinations safely.

The lighthouse has been there a lot longer than its neighbor. The light tower dates to 1899, while the bridge is of far more recent construction. Unfortunately, whereas the Jamestown Bridge receives regular maintenance, the lighthouse looks its age—every

bit the centenarian. Despite its age and run-down condition, however, the Plum Beach spark-plug tower is a tough old lighthouse. It was built to take a beating and has withstood many storms and even a few hurricanes.

Construction of the open-water tower was completed in several stages. First a large caisson was built and sunk over the site. Then the water was pumped out, allowing work to progress in relatively dry conditions. High-pressure pumps continuously removed the water, sand, and muck that leaked into the construction caisson.

The completed station received a fourth-order Fresnel lens, initially powered by kerosene lamps. Electric power soon replaced the kerosene. The Plum Beach Light guided mariners for more than forty years. It was deactivated in 1941, when the lights of the newly built Jamestown Bridge rendered it obsolete.

Since that time the lighthouse has stood alone and more or less forgotten to face the elements on its own. The question now is whether the old light tower will continue its deterioration until it finally collapses into the bay. Thanks to a large number of local lighthouse friends and avid preservationists, it will likely be saved.

Restoration efforts were delayed for many years by an extraordinary lawsuit that dragged on for decades. In 1973 Rhode Island officials employed a Newport man to paint the rusty Plum Beach tower. The painter contracted a serious eye disease, allegedly from the thick layer of pigeon droppings that coated the tower. Having lost some of his vision, the painter sued the state. The state denied ownership, but a 1998 Superior Court decision ruled against it, forcing a settlement of the suit and opening the door for transfer of the property to the Friends of Plum Beach Lighthouse. This nonprofit organization hopes to restore the station to its former glory.

Lighthouse Digest

The Plum Beach Lighthouse stands on its caisson in the west passage of Rhode Island's Narragansett Bay.

AVERY POINT LIGHTHOUSE
Groton, Connecticut

1942

The University of Connecticut maintains an attractive satellite campus in Groton near the mouth of the fabled Connecticut River. Before it was a college campus, the property served as an important Coast Guard base. The gorgeous land hereabouts was once part of the expansive estate of the well-known industrialist, philanthropist, and yachtsman Morton Plant. After Plant died in 1938, the estate passed first to the state of Connecticut and then to the U.S. Coast Guard for use as a wartime training facility.

During the early 1940s the Coast Guard built the small Avery Point Lighthouse tower on the training center lawn facing the river and the open waters of Long Island Sound. Although it was lighted for a time as a private navigational aid, the little brick tower was never meant to guide ships. Instead it was intended to serve as a reminder of the Coast Guard's lighthouse-keeping responsibilities and, perhaps, as a memorial to the men and women who dedicated their lives to keep the nation's navigational lights burning. So it is especially ironic that this light tower is now in danger.

When the Coast Guard closed the Groton training center in 1967, the memorial light was snuffed out. Afterward little or no maintenance was done on the stone tower. Today it stands in a sad state of disrepair. The university is now in charge of the property, but like other educational institutions, it is hard-pressed financially and has no money to spend on "frills" such as the Avery Point Lighthouse. The estimated cost of refurbishing the tower ranges upwards of $100,000. The American Lighthouse Foundation is helping a local preservation group raise the necessary funds to restore the lighthouse.

Dale Treadway

Built during the 1940s as a memorial, the Avery Point Lighthouse in Groton was never a key navigational marker.

The photograph below shows the damage done to the structure by weathering and time.

KEEP OUT
HAZARDOUS AREA

Dale Treadway

FAULKNER'S ISLAND LIGHTHOUSE

Near Guilford, Connecticut

Commissioned by President Thomas Jefferson in 1802, the Faulkner's Island Lighthouse near Guilford is Connecticut's second oldest navigational station. Only the venerable New London Harbor Light, established in 1760, is older. Despite its obvious historic merit, however, the two-centuries-old Faulkner's Island tower may soon be lost, a victim of erosion and—strangely enough—rabbits.

Thousands of years ago glaciers sculpted a four-acre, crescent-shaped island a few miles off the mainland of what is now Connecticut. Faulkner's Island lies at the center of a veritable minefield of rocks strung out along the Connecticut shore. The lighthouse was built to warn vessels against the danger, which is considerable. Hundreds of vessels were lost here, and the carnage continued even after the light atop the 40-foot stone tower began to shine. Joseph

Faulkner's Island Light Station in the aftermath of a disastrous fire in 1976. The blaze destroyed the century-old keeper's residence and blackened the stone walls of the octagonal tower.

22

Griffing had only recently moved to the island and taken over as the station's first keeper when he found the bodies of seven shipwrecked sailors washed up on the Faulkner's Island beach. He buried the men on a small neighboring island.

Griffing and other early keepers did the best they could to warn mariners, but they were handicapped by the limitations of their whale-oil lamps and reflectors. After 1856 the Faulkner's Island beacon got a boost from a newly installed fourth-order Fresnel lens, which gave the light added range and visibility. The fine, French-made glass lens remained in service for more than 120 years. It was finally replaced by a modern, aeromarine optic when the station was automated in 1978. The station's rambling, two-and-a-half-story keeper's quarters had burned to the ground just two years earlier.

Fortunately the historic stone tower was a detached structure, and it survived the blaze. Now the tower itself is threatened. The waters off Long Island Sound are cutting closer and closer to the foundation. Unless something is done, the erosion will eventually undercut the foundation and dump the tower into the sound.

Strangely enough the erosion has been hastened by the small army of rabbits that now run wild over the property. The rabbits are not native to Faulkner's Island. They were introduced by a former keeper who turned loose a pair of pet rabbits rather than take them with him when he returned to the mainland. The abandoned, long-eared pets then proceeded to breed like—you get the idea. The rabbits are constantly burrowing to create their proverbial holes, and, in doing so, they weaken the island soil, making it more vulnerable to erosion.

Fortunately for the tower and for lighthouse lovers everywhere, the Faulkner's Island Light has plenty of friends. A local group of preservationist stalwarts, known as the Faulkner's Island Light Brigade, is determined to save the structure. In addition to raising money privately, the group has received funds from both state and federal grants. The funding has been used to completely restore the tower and to begin an erosion control project.

Faulkner's Island is now populated only by wildlife, including a number of rabbits. These descendants of pet rabbits turned loose by a former keeper have weakened the soil with their constant burrowing.

PLUM ISLAND LIGHTHOUSE

Near Orient Point, New York

1827

They weren't known as U.S. Marines back then, but in August of 1775 a small force of Continental soldiers attacked a British force on Plum Island in a manner likely to make any leatherneck beam with pride—they stormed ashore under fire. This may have been America's first successful amphibious assault. There were no lights on hand to guide the Continental landing craft, but if it had arrived fifty-two years later, there might have been.

In 1827 the government established a light station on Plum Island to help sailors traverse the treacherous, swift-running waters of Plum Gut off the far northeastern end of Long Island. Tidal currents often race through the gut at speeds of up to six knots. To successfully navigate these dangerous narrows, mariners must know where they are at all times.

The original Plum Island Lighthouse had an octagonal, rough-stone tower approximately 30 feet tall. The lantern room was equipped with a patented Winslow Lewis lamp and reflector system, which did not always work well. The brightness and range of the beacon increased considerably in 1856 when the tower received a fourth-order Fresnel lens. However, the addition of the new lens could do nothing to shore up the failing structural integrity of the lighthouse itself. Built under the tutelage of a notoriously parsimonious government official, the Plum Island Lighthouse had been constructed on a very tight budget—that is to say, as cheaply as possible.

The Lighthouse Board, which in 1852 took charge of all American light stations, inspected the Plum Island facility in 1868 and found it to be falling apart. By the following year it had been replaced by a much better built, two-story granite structure with a tower and lantern rising from its roof. Made to last, the 1868 lighthouse still stands today, more than 130 years after its last stone was placed.

Although its walls remain rock solid, the Plum Island Lighthouse needs help. In 1979 the nearby Orient Point Light was upgraded, enabling its beacon to cover much of Plum Gut. This made the Plum Island Light more or less redundant, and it was extinguished. Since that time only minimal maintenance has been done on the old tower. Today the lighthouse is threatened by erosion, which brings the waters of the sound closer with every passing year. Erosion has already destroyed the station's generator house, which fell into the sea in 1997.

A local preservationist organization, known as the East End Seaport Lighthouse Committee, hopes to save the historic lighthouse. Funds raised by the committee will be used first to halt the erosion and then to restore the building so that it can be opened to the public. Standing in the way of this plan is the U.S. Agriculture Department, which maintains a research station on the 840-acre island. In 1999 it was announced that the government might soon be conducting biological warfare research on Plum Island.

The waters of Long Island Sound have placed the 1868 Plum Island Lighthouse under siege. Each year erosion brings the waves nearer to its granite walls. A local committee is fighting to save the historic building.

Lighthouse Digest

CEDAR ISLAND LIGHTHOUSE
Near Sag Harbor, New York

1868

When the Long Island whaling fleet returned home from the sea, its homesick sailors were greeted by an American flag flying from the lighthouse at Cedar Point near Sag Harbor. Keepers of this eastern Long Island light station made a habit of hoisting a flag whenever they spotted ships inbound from the Atlantic.

The station was established in 1839 on a low, three-acre island that was then cloaked in a distinctive grove of tall cedars. Over time the shifting sands of Long Island Sound filled in the 200 yards of shallows separating it from the mainland, and Cedar Island became Cedar Point. Even so, the navigational station retained its original name: Cedar Island Lighthouse.

In 1868 the original Cedar Island Lighthouse, a rather modest structure, was replaced with the more imposing edifice that stands today. The contractor, the W & J Beattie Company of Fall River, Massachusetts, owned a granite quarry, and built the lighthouse of granite. A handsome, two-story Victorian structure with a lantern perched atop a brick tower attached to the house, it closely resembled several other lighthouses built at about this same time.

The lantern was equipped with a sixth-order Fresnel lens, which combined with the 40-foot elevation of the lantern room to give the beacon a range of about 11 miles. Later the small sixth-order lens gave way to a more powerful fourth-order lens, which no doubt boosted the range of the light considerably. In 1882 the station received a mechanical fog signal.

The Cedar Island Lighthouse as it looks today. The tall steel tower that now marks the approach to Sag Harbor can be seen in the background on the right.

Robert G. Muller

Robert G. Muller

The wanton destruction of mindless vandalism can be seen in these photographs. Vandals are not just bored thrill seekers—they are criminals. Like other thieves, they take what is not theirs, and in the case of historic buildings, objects stolen or destroyed may never be replaced.

Appointed keeper in 1897 was Charles Mumford, the scion of an old Sag Harbor sailing family. Mumford had been maimed during the Civil War, and for nearly ten years he thumped around the station on a wooden leg. Apparently Mumford did quite a bit of walking, since he kept a stack of spare legs on hand in the attic of the lighthouse. Firefighters came across a pile of Mumford's blackened and smoldering spares after a blaze swept through the structure in 1974.

The Cedar Island Lighthouse dependably guided mariners until 1934, when its duties were passed along to an automated light on a nearby 57-foot steel tower. Not long afterwards, the U.S. Treasury Department declared the lighthouse surplus property and auctioned it off for a mere $2,000. This less than modest price indicates the low value once placed—

and in too many instances still placed—on retired lighthouses.

What happened to this lovely and historic building after it was sold is likewise characteristic of the fate of abandoned lighthouses. Battered by wind and weather, it quickly became dilapidated. Vandals had their way with the building and in 1974 set fire to it. The blaze destroyed the roof, gutted the oak interior, and cracked the walls. Since then efforts to restore the lighthouse or even to save it from further deterioration have been insufficient. One well-meaning campaign raised so little money that it could not even pay the cost of its own publicity posters. A new group, called Friends of Cedar Island Lighthouse, has recently been formed to assess the condition of the lighthouse and stabilize the structure. The group's long-term goal is a complete restoration.

NORTH BROTHER ISLAND LIGHTHOUSE
New York City

ery little remains of the North Brother Island Lighthouse that once guarded Hell Gate, a key passage linking New York City's East River with the open waters of Long Island Sound. The 50-foot tower that once held aloft the station's fourth-order Fresnel lens is gone, and the square wooden residence is deteriorating rapidly.

Built in 1869, the lighthouse was relatively small, but comfortable and well equipped. The building contained a kitchen, pantry, dining room, and sitting room, as well as four bedrooms and an oil storage area. The doors and windows of the lighthouse were boarded up after the Coast Guard abandoned the property in 1953. Efforts are now under way, however, to restore and relight the old beacon.

The North Brother Island station was witness to many fascinating and, in some cases, tragic events. On June 15, 1904, the excursion and party ship *General Slocum* caught fire not far from North Brother Island and its lighthouse. The vessel was crowded with New Yorkers who had gone out for an early summer afternoon cruise. For most it would be their last boat ride. The ship quickly turned into a floating torch, and although the North Brother Island keepers and assistants tried to help, little if anything could be done. More than a thousand lives were lost in this early-twentieth-century calamity—the worst maritime disaster in New York history.

Adjacent to the lighthouse was the Riverside Hospital where the notorious (Typhoid) Mary Mallon was once incarcerated. Although immune to typhoid, she carried the deadly disease and spread it to dozens, if not hundreds, of New Yorkers. Mary was arrested and committed to the hospital after she refused to stop working as a cook.

Built in 1869, the North Brother Island Lighthouse marked New York's Hell Gate for more than eighty years. (Inset) Abandoned in 1953, the station has fallen into ruin. The tower has collapsed into the keeper's house and most likely it is too late to save this important reminder of New York's maritime history.

FORT WADSWORTH LIGHTHOUSE
New York City

1903

One of America's smallest lighthouses stands in the shadow of one of the world's largest bridges. A tiny tower perched atop an antiquated stone fort, it can be seen on the eastern shore of Staten Island, not far from where the hulking Verrazano-Narrows Bridge completes its nearly 2-mile crossing. A simple brick platform, little larger than a storage shed, holds the small, crosshatched iron lantern.

Of course size can be deceiving. The little light station's light—now extinguished—was far more important than the diminutive stature of its abandoned tower suggests. The high walls of the fort lifted the flashing fourth-order beacon some 75 feet above sea level, from which elevation it could be seen from the decks of every ship bound for the crowded wharves of New York City. Countless mariners depended on this light to guide them safely through the narrows. The Fort Wadsworth Station

served until 1963, when construction of the huge bridge—itself a sort of lighthouse—rendered it obsolete. Now abandoned and rusted, the little lighthouse seems in danger of being forgotten altogether.

Lighthouse Digest by Peter Elbert

Its lens and windows removed long ago, the station's rusted iron lantern is rapidly deteriorating.

U.S. Coast Guard

Grass grew on top of Fort Wadsworth when this photograph was taken early in the twentieth century. A quite modest structure, the lighthouse was nonetheless vital to mariners.

Lighthouse Digest by Dana Elbert

Placed on the walls of the stone defense works guarding the seaward approaches to New York City, the Fort Wadsworth Lighthouse marked the strategic Verrazano Narrows.

ESOPUS MEADOWS LIGHTHOUSE

Near Esopus, New York

1871

*I*n 1838 the village of Esopus, New York, sold the U.S. government an important parcel of land for the price of a single greenback. By most estimates the property was worth even less than that, since it was located right in the middle of the Hudson River and, most of the time, was actually underwater. But for river pilots navigating this stretch of the Hudson, about 100 miles north of New York City, it was a key piece of real estate. It was the perfect place for a lighthouse, and one was desperately needed.

Just west of the parcel, the Hudson opens onto a broad expanse of mudflats known locally as Esopus Meadows. These shallows represent a significant threat to shipping, and more than a few vessels have come to grief here. During the late 1830s a light-house was built on piles driven into the thick mud of the Esopus parcel. For thirty years it warned vessels away from the meadows, but constant battering by floods and ice eventually left it a useless wreck. In 1871 it was demolished and replaced by the current lighthouse. The lighthouse has now been leased to the Save Esopus Lighthouse Commission. The group has completed structural engineering and architectural surveys, and has done emergency repairs.

To give the new light station a more secure foundation, a forest of 250 piles was driven deep into the riverbed. The piles were capped with 12-inch timbers and planked over with pine, creating a platform almost 50 feet wide. Atop the platform workmen built a two-story, seven-room clapboard residence consisting of a kitchen, dining room, sitting room,

The now endangered Esopus Meadows Lighthouse once warned vessels away from river shoals and shallows.

The station was closed in 1965, and the years since have been very hard on the seven-room, combination tower and dwelling. Time has been at war with these walls.

A staircase in need of paint and a good carpenter.

several bedrooms, and a 25-foot light tower. The lantern room held a fifth-order Fresnel lens, and its light shined out over the Hudson from an elevation 58 feet above mean low water.

Protected by a massive granite wall, the Esopus Meadows Lighthouse (also known as the Middle Hudson River Lighthouse) has survived the river's destructive floods and ice floes for more than 130 years, but there is now some question as to how much longer it can stand. Since the last full-time keepers were removed in 1965, the wooden, Victorian-style structure has deteriorated markedly. The worst threat to the building is the uneven settling that has left the east side some 16 inches higher than the west. The settling places considerable strain on the structure and may cause it to collapse.

Preservationists hope to move the lighthouse to a new set of piles driven into a more stable stretch of river bottom. Money is being raised to finance the move and restore the tower and residence. As recently as 1998 the Coast Guard announced that the historic building would be dynamited unless the funds needed to save it were raised.

No one tends to this stove—or the sagging ceiling and roof above it.

MISPILLION LIGHTHOUSE
Near Milford, Delaware

1873 OR 1875

On the banks of Delaware's Mispillion Creek stands a most unusual lighthouse, unlike any other in America. Most U.S. lighthouses were built according to plans drawn up and approved by government officials, but the Mispillion Lighthouse was designed and built entirely by local craftsmen.

Located beside the broad Delaware Bay about 12 miles from Milford, the Mispillion Light Station was intended to mark the entrance to the creek and help guide vessels passing through the bay on their way to Philadelphia or the open Atlantic. The station did its job so poorly, however, that it was discontinued in 1857. The original lighthouse, built by the well-known government contractor Winslow Lewis for only $1,500, was sold to a private owner who moved it to Milford for use as a residence.

Complaints from local fisherman and other maritime interests led to reestablishment of the light during the 1870s. According to the rather sketchy surviving records, the lighthouse placed here in 1872 was either substantially enlarged or completely rebuilt in 1875. Since that time the wood-frame building has changed very little. A modest two-story dwelling and attached, square wooden tower approximately 48-feet tall, it is a remarkable hodgepodge of styles and construction techniques. Its walls are covered by board-and-batten siding in some places, composite or wood shingles in others, and metal siding in still others. The small iron lantern atop the tower looks quite out of place.

The entire building was thrown together for only about $5,000 with an additional $4,000 being spent some years later to protect the site from flooding and erosion. All in all, the U.S. Treasury got a good deal on the little lighthouse, especially considering that it served mariners and the public for more than sixty years. Produced by a small, sixth-order Fresnel lens, the station's beacon guided traffic on the bay until 1929, when the task was handed over to an automated light shining from a nearby utilitarian steel skeleton tower.

Remarkably, despite dry rot, weathering, floods, powerful gales, and even hurricanes, the Mispillion Lighthouse still stands. While in need of considerable repair, it has well-wishers who would like to see it restored and saved. As of 1999 it was part of a parcel of private property that included an adjacent marina and bayside restaurant.

Lighthouse Digest

The Mispillion Lighthouse, about 12 miles from Milford, was the work of local craftsmen.

FISHING BATTERY LIGHTHOUSE

Near Havre de Grace, Maryland

1853

In the far northern reaches of the Chesapeake Bay, not far from the mouth of the Susquehanna River, stand the intriguing remnants of a nearly 150-year-old light station. Established in 1853, it was known as the Fishing Battery Lighthouse, and for many years it marked the entrance to the river. During the late nineteenth century, the U.S. Bureau of Fisheries set up a small facility here for studying the Chesapeake's commercial fish population.

The lighthouse was thought to have been demolished when its beacon was automated in 1921, but not so. The two-story brick structure survives, even though its base is all but awash in the waters of the bay. Perched on its roof is the same small lantern that once held a sixth-order Fresnel lens. The structure is in dilapidated condition and its walls bear marks of vandalism. Some Chesapeake pleasure boaters who have visited the site believe it may be repairable. The Chesapeake Heritage Conservancy is looking into the possible restoration of the lighthouse.

Maryland's Fishing Battery Lighthouse still stands nearly eight decades after it was supposed to have been demolished. Seen behind the brick structure is the steel skeleton tower that took over the task of marking the Susquehanna River entrance in 1921.

Lighthouse Digest

FORT CARROLL LIGHTHOUSE

Near Baltimore, Maryland

1854

Every day thousands of motorists jam Baltimore's Francis Scott Key Bridge. Most are unaware that only about a mile east of the bridge a massive chunk of history rises from the waters of Chesapeake Bay. Unlike Fort McHenry, which is located much closer to the heart of downtown Baltimore, Fort Carroll was never celebrated in poetry or song. It was never attacked by a British fleet. In fact, it was never even completed. But the antique fortress is nonetheless quite historic.

Beginning in 1847 Robert E. Lee, then a colonel in the U.S. Army Corps of Engineers, supervised the construction of Fort Carroll's granite walls. Lee spent almost three years and more than $1 million in federal funds trying to complete the four-acre fort. It was supposed to have 40-foot-high walls and hold 350 powerful cannon. However, only the lower part of the fort was ever built, and Congress gave up on the project long before it was finished. By 1851 Lee had departed to take up his post as superintendent of the U.S. Military Academy at West Point. Later on he would pass into legend as commander of the Confederate Army of Northern Virginia.

The unfinished fort played no direct military role in the Civil War, but it did serve an important strategic purpose by guiding ships up the Patapsco River toward the vital port facilities at Baltimore. In 1854 a tiny lighthouse had been erected on one of Fort Carroll's parapets. For many years the only occupant of the huge fort was the light's lonely keeper.

In 1898, during the Spanish-American War, Fort Carroll at long last received a military garrison, albeit a small one. A pair of shore batteries were put in place on top of the old walls, and soldiers were assigned to man them. To make room for the guns, the lighthouse was torn down and rebuilt about 100 feet from the batteries. All this was done on the rather preposterous assumption that Spanish ships might bull their way up the Chesapeake and attack Baltimore. No such assault ever materialized, and the guns were eventually removed.

Fort Carroll's shore batteries are long gone, but astoundingly its tiny wooden light tower still stands. The lantern at the top of the boxy, two-story structure once held a fifth-order Fresnel lens, and its light, shining from a point some 45 feet above the water, could reach vessels far out in Chesapeake Bay. Today, however, the lantern is empty. The tower was abandoned when its light was deactivated shortly after World War II. Like the rest of Fort Carroll, it now has a neglected and ghostly appearance.

Over the years there have been several plans to restore the fort and its lighthouse. So far no practical restoration work has been done. Wild shrubs and trees have run rampant, and every year their roots dig deeper into the crumbling walls. The Fort Carroll Preservation Trust is now hoping to preserve the fort and the lighthouse before time runs out.

Lighthouse Digest

This small wooden tower served as a key navigational marker for many years. Now it and the Fort Carroll walls on which it stands are threatened by weather, water, and the march of time.

SHARP'S ISLAND LIGHTHOUSE

Chesapeake Bay, south of Tighman Island

1882

As if it had struck a shoal and sprung a leak, the Sharp's Island Lighthouse has developed a dramatic list. Although it appears to be about to slip beneath the waters of Chesapeake Bay, the 120-year-old caisson-type lighthouse is in no danger of sinking. Even so, unless some action is taken to save it, and soon, this familiar Chesapeake seamark may very well vanish.

Rather than pay the estimated $55,000 cost of stabilizing the open water tower and bear the considerable annual expense of maintenance, Coast Guard officials would prefer to remove it. A demolition plan has been under discussion since 1996. However, public protest has so far blocked the plan, and the tower may, in time, be rescued—perhaps by being towed to the grounds of a park or museum.

If the lighthouse cannot be saved, it will follow a long line of other Chesapeake light stations into oblivion. Scores of navigational lights once served the bay, and many of them have been swept away by storms, ice, human hands, or time. In fact two earlier lighthouses marked Sharp's Island—named for a Quaker who settled here in the seventeenth century. The first of these, built in 1838, was undercut by erosion and removed shortly after the Civil War. The second, a cottage-style structure, was knocked off its screw-pile foundation and carried down the bay by an 1881 ice jam. It is easy to understand why government officials had the current tower built on a massive caisson. Most caisson towers have proven impervious to ice, but the Sharp's Island Lighthouse finally yielded to a giant floe during the 1970s and has suffered from its list ever since.

Known to many nowadays as "the leaning tower of the Chesapeake," the caisson-style Sharp's Island Lighthouse remains in operation. Knocked sideways by an ice floe during the 1970s, it now displays a dramatic list. Even so, it continues to guide ships.

ENDANGERED TOWERS OF THE SOUTH

North Carolina to Texas

Endangered Towers of the South

North Carolina

• Bodie Island

Price's Creek

South Carolina

Morris Island

Georgia

Little Cumberland Island

Mississippi

Alabama

Atlantic Ocean

Texas

Louisiana

• Sand Island

West Rigolets   Cape St. George

Galveston   Ship Shoal
Jetty   Pass a l'Outre   Florida
       Sabine Bank   Frank's Island   Anclote Key
                                     Southwest Pass
Sabine Pass

Gulf
of Mexico

N

BODIE ISLAND LIGHTHOUSE
Bodie Island, North Carolina

1872

The successful relocation of the Cape Hatteras Lighthouse has focused attention on endangered light towers across the country. Among these threatened structures is Hatteras's nearby sister on Bodie Island in the North Carolina Outer Banks. But where erosion was the problem at Cape Hatteras, the enemy of the Bodie Island Lighthouse is simply old age.

According to a study completed several years ago by the Outer Banks Lighthouse Society, the lantern room and gallery deck showed clear signs of decay.

Timothy Harrison

Corrosion had all but consumed the original metal fixtures holding the deck in place.

A more recent report prepared by the National Park Service declared the tower unsafe and unstable due to significant and extensive deterioration. The ironwork and staircase were found to be in a critical state of disrepair, with cracked or broken sections throughout the structure. The fine old first-order Fresnel lens at the top of the Bodie tower was also found in need of restoration.

Help may be coming to the Bodie Island Lighthouse, but will it arrive in time? The National Park Service has put together a nearly $2 million plan to restore the lighthouse and its lens, but it could be as late as 2002 before the Park Service can include the Bodie funding in its budget request to Congress.

The Bodie Island Lighthouse lays claim to a history almost as dramatic and fascinating as that of the more famous Hatteras tower a few dozen miles to the south. The existing Bodie Island tower dates to 1872, making it almost as old as Hatteras (1870). Two earlier towers stood on this site. The first was built in 1847. The second, completed in 1859, was blown up by Confederate forces during the Civil War to keep it out of Union hands.

Restoring the Bodie Island Lighthouse will save it for the wonder and enjoyment of future generations. Many visitors find the Bodie tower, with its broad black-and-white bands, an especially inspiring sight. Perhaps in time visitors will once again climb the tower's 242 spiraling stairs (now closed to the public) to enjoy a sweeping view of the Atlantic once known only to lighthouse keepers.

When approaching from the north, Bodie Island Lighthouse is the first building most visitors see within the Cape Hatteras National Seashore. The tower's magnificent appearance is deceiving, however. Most who see and appreciate it from a distance are unaware of its deteriorating condition.

PRICE'S CREEK LIGHTHOUSE
Near Southport, North Carolina

1848

A sparkling string of navigational lights once marked the Cape Fear River from the Atlantic as far west as Wilmington, some 25 miles inland. The only relic of this impressive river light system is the Price's Creek Lighthouse, which now lies in ruins not far from Southport. The brick walls of the tower can be seen, but nothing else of the station remains.

In 1848 Congress appropriated funds for modest lighthouse stations to be established at Price's Creek, Campbell's Island, Orton's Point, and Oak Point, all along the Cape Fear River. Except for the ruins at Price's Creek, all these stations have been swept away by weather, war, and time. Records suggest that most were discontinued either during or shortly after the Civil War.

The Price's Creek Lighthouse had a tower some 20 feet high and 3 feet thick. As recently as 1917 the lantern cage remained in place, but it has vanished since. Now located on private property, the tower itself may soon disappear.

National Archives

Bob & Sandra Shanklin, "The Lighthouse People"

This ghostly old photograph dates to 1917, when the lantern cage was still in place on the Price's Creek tower.

The tower today. Although dark for more than a century, its light once guided ships along the Cape Fear River to Wilmington, North Carolina.

MORRIS ISLAND LIGHTHOUSE

Charleston, South Carolina

1876

ew lighthouses anywhere in North America can lay claim to more history than the one on Morris Island near the harbor entrance of Charleston, South Carolina. The light station dates all the way back to 1767, when South Carolina was a colony of Great Britain. The first battle of the Civil War was fought practically in the shadow of the mighty Morris Island tower as Confederate artillerymen opened up on nearby Fort Sumter. Blown up during the war, the original Charleston sentinel was replaced by the current tower in 1876.

Having survived floods, fires, and hurricanes, as well as the calamitous 1886 Charleston earthquake, the banded, 155-foot tower still stands, but no one can say for how long. Just as Union troops once assaulted Charleston, the ocean has now placed this immensely historic building under siege. In fact, Morris Island itself has disappeared. Home to generations of keepers and their families, it was swallowed up by the tidal surges of hurricanes early in the twentieth century. Salt water now laps the tower foundation from every direction of the compass.

The fact that the Morris Island tower survives at all is a testament to the quality of its workmanship. It took almost four years to complete and cost $150,000—a considerable sum during the 1870s. To provide a sound foundation, 264 piles were driven deep into the island sands and underlying mud, creating a circle with a radius of 22 feet. The piles were capped with timber, concrete, and masonry, and the 3,200-ton brick tower was erected on top.

The structure's enormous mass may have helped it weather Hurricane Hugo, which devastated much of Charleston in 1979. Whether it will stand up to the next great hurricane is anyone's guess. Both private groups and public agencies are attempting to piece together the funds needed to save and restore the lighthouse. A complete restoration may cost millions of dollars.

A local citizens group called Save the Lighthouse recently purchased the tower for $75,000 from its private owners and then sold it to the state of South Carolina. The state then leased the tower to Save the Lighthouse. This unusual procedure made the lighthouse eligible for the government funding needed to save it. The Army Corps of Engineers has agreed to spend up to $1 million for a stabilization study.

Lighthouse Digest

Surrounded by water, the historic Morris Island Lighthouse tower near Charleston remains upright, still balanced on its 264 piles. But for how long? Hurricane-driven flood tides swept away the surrounding island and keeper's residence many years ago.

LITTLE CUMBERLAND ISLAND LIGHTHOUSE

Near Brunswick, Georgia

1838

*I*ts crumbling brick walls enveloped by a lush coastal forest, the Little Cumberland Island Lighthouse possesses all the majesty and mystery of a Mayan temple rising above the canopy of a rain forest. Although not an ancient ruin, the nineteenth-century light tower is nonetheless an evocative reminder of times long past. Built in 1838, a generation before the Civil War, it served mariners until 1915, shortly after the outbreak of World War I.

Located on a mostly wild and swampy island near the far southern end of Georgia's Atlantic coast, the Little Cumberland Island station marked the entrance to St. Andrews Sound a few miles south of Brunswick. Early keepers were local farmers who earned a little extra income by tending the light. For many years the station's fixed beacon was produced by oil lamps fitted with polished reflectors. Later a third-order Fresnel lens would focus the light.

Unlike many other southern lighthouses, this one survived the Civil War more or less intact. A report filed shortly after the war suggests that retreating Confederate forces may have done some minor damage to the station. Whatever it was, the damage was repaired and the light was put back in full-time service by 1867.

After the Lighthouse Service abandoned the station in 1915, the tower stood empty and neglected for more than half a century. Even so, its 60-foot-high brick walls were still in remarkably good condition when a property owners' association took control of the island during the 1960s. In 1968 the Little Cumberland association spent $5,000 to shore up and repair the tower. Additional maintenance has been done since that time, but the lighthouse is still in danger.

Bob & Sandra Shanklin, "The Lighthouse People"

Abandoned more than eighty-five years ago, the Little Cumberland Island Lighthouse once marked Georgia's St. Andrews Sound. Some restoration work has been done by the island's private owners' association. Although homes have been built on Little Cumberland, most of the island remains undeveloped. The brick light tower rises above some of its wildest acreage.

ANCLOTE KEY LIGHTHOUSE
Near Tarpon Springs, Florida

1887

To the west of Tampa, a line of low, sandy barrier islands forms a wall separating the Florida coast from the open waters of the Gulf of Mexico. At the northern end of the chain, not far from the fishing village of Tarpon Springs, is Anclote Key. Except for its decaying light station, the key remains undeveloped and appears today much as all of Florida must have looked before the arrival of the first European settlers. The swampy key is now a protected wildlife refuge, and, sure enough, wild things—mosquitoes in particular—seem far more at home there than people. Likely, it has always been so.

In 1682 a fleet of pirate ships dropped anchor off Anclote Key, and a small navy of 400 or more buccaneers made the place a base for raids up and down the Gulf coast. Although the Spanish authorities in Florida failed to drive the marauders away, the prodigious swarms of Anclote mosquitoes and other biting insects soon routed them. Within a few months, the pirates had set sail, never to return.

More than two centuries would pass before the key was put to legitimate use—as the site of an important coastal lighthouse. Completed in 1887 at a cost of approximately $35,000, the Anclote Key Light Station consisted of a 96-foot steel skeleton tower as well as a residence and storage buildings. From the lantern room, a third-order Fresnel lens flashed out the station's red warning beacon at intervals of thirty seconds.

Keepers assigned to Anclote frequently complained of the mosquitoes, but unlike the pirates who had come here so many years earlier, they could not board their vessels and move along to another, less buggy place. However, the keepers and their families did make frequent trips across the short 2-mile stretch of sheltered water separating the island from the mainland. Nearly every week they visited the village of Anclote or nearby Tarpon Springs to pick up supplies and, no doubt, lay in stocks of insect repellent.

The Anclote Lighthouse guided ships, fishing boats, and pleasure craft along the Florida coast for almost a century. Its beacon went dark in 1984, and the property became part of a state park. Unfortunately little has been done to protect the tower, which is at the mercy of vandals. Walls have been defaced and bricks stolen from station buildings.

Money has been raised locally for the purpose of refurbishing the lighthouse and, perhaps, restoring its beacon, but to date the fund remains far less than sufficient. In 1999 the Florida legislature set aside $1.25 million for restoration of the Anclote Lighthouse, but the bill was vetoed by the governor.

The skeleton tower of Anclote Key Lighthouse rises above the swampy wilderness. Thieves have stolen bricks from the ruins of the station residence and oil house.

CAPE ST. GEORGE LIGHTHOUSE

Near Apalachicola, Florida

1852

A venerable monument to the Old South cotton trade that once brought river steamboats and oceangoing freighters to Apalachicola, the Cape St. George Lighthouse may yet be gone with the wind. Repeatedly battered by hurricanes and undercut by rampaging beach erosion, this Florida panhandle sentinel developed a pronounced lean, and for decades it seemed on the point of collapse. A costly stabilization project, completed early in 2000, has partially corrected the lean and may have pulled the old tower back from the edge of extinction. Even so, it remains seriously threatened and may very well fall in the next powerful storm.

Established in 1833 to facilitate the Gulf coast cotton trade, the original Cape St. George Lighthouse was the work of legendary contractor Winslow Lewis. A former New England sea captain, Lewis was not a trained engineer. Working within a no-frills budget of $9,500, he built the station's 72-foot brick tower, equipping it with one of his own patented lamp-and-reflector lighting systems. Notoriously unreliable, the Lewis reflectors worked no better here than elsewhere, and the light could be seen from only a few miles out at sea. On more than one occasion, ships slammed into the nearby shallows without ever having spotted the beacon. Nonetheless, no telling improvements were made until the early 1850s, when an entirely new lighthouse was built here.

The existing lighthouse dates to 1852, when it was built on orders of the recently commissioned Lighthouse Board. Composed of military officers, professional engineers, and maritime experts, the Board launched a massive effort to upgrade all of America's lighthouses. The light station at Cape St. George was given a stout brick tower and a state-of-the-art Fresnel lens, which gave the light an improved range of more than 15 miles.

Apparently the new tower was very well constructed. It has lasted through dozens of hurricanes, countless gales, and even an attack by Confederate artillery. No structure, however, can stand for long when the ground is cut from under it, and this is what has happened at Cape St. George. The sands along the Gulf are in constant motion, and they have brought the waters within a few feet of the light tower. In fact, at high tide the foundation is often awash.

In an attempt to save the tower, engineers have stabilized its sand base and partially corrected its lean. A series of 18-inch holes have been bored into the lower walls and refilled with fiberglass and concrete to redistribute the weight. Other structures at the station appear to be beyond help.

Recently straightened and stabilized, the leaning tower at Cape St. George appears to be out of danger, at least for the moment. As this picture makes only too clear, other structures are beyond repair.

Bob & Sandra Shanklin, "The Lighthouse People"

SAND ISLAND LIGHTHOUSE

Near Mobile, Alabama

1871

The state of Alabama and the entire Gulf coast may be in danger of losing their most dramatic coastal symbol. The 125-foot brick tower of the Sand Island Lighthouse has boldly marked the entrance to Mobile Bay since 1871. Its light was snuffed out by the Coast Guard many years ago, but during the day the old tower can still be seen from miles in every direction. Coastal residents wonder how much longer this may be the case.

In 1973 the two-story residence that stood beside the tower for nearly half a century burned to the ground. Six years later Hurricane Frederick carried away not only the ruins of the dwelling but the entire island. Only the tower remained, standing tall above its protective ballast stones and riprap. Will the next big storm take the tower as well?

For a century the Sand Island Light Station guided mariners along the Gulf coast and into the bay. The island's first sentinel, a relatively modest 52-foot tower, was completed in 1838. It served until 1859, when it was replaced by a magnificent 150-foot brick giant fitted with the finest available Fresnel lens. Grand though it was, the new lighthouse was to have a very short service life—less than two years. In 1861 Confederate raiders blew it up to keep it from being used by Union Army observers.

Not until several years after the Civil War did work commence on a replacement. Foundation stones were finally laid in July of 1872, but it would take more than a year for masons to complete the lofty brick cylinder. The new light began operation on September 1, 1873. Although struck repeatedly by powerful gales and hurricanes, the lighthouse guided shipping more or less continuously for sixty years. It was finally taken out of service in 1933.

National Archives

U.S. Coast Guard

(Left) The Civil War–era Sand Island Lighthouse a year or so before it was destroyed by Confederate troops in 1861. Ironically the raiders assigned to blow up the tower reported their success to Danville Leadbetter, by then a Confederate official. Just three years earlier, Leadbetter had designed the structure and supervised its construction for the U.S. government. (Right) The abandoned Sand Island Lighthouse as it looked about 1950. The two-story dwelling on the right burned in 1973.

WEST RIGOLETS LIGHTHOUSE

West Rigolets, Louisiana

1855

It now looks much like a ramshackle bayou fisherman's hut, but the West Rigolets Lighthouse was once vital to Louisiana commerce. Built in 1855, it marked a key passage linking the Gulf of Mexico to Lake Ponchartrain and the bustling markets of New Orleans. The Union and Confederacy fought over the station during the Civil War. In fact, a keeper here, shot to death during a Southern raid, was the only active Lighthouse Service employee killed during the war.

Built on piles and held above the brackish lake waters by wooden stilts, the station consisted of a small dwelling with a tiny lantern positioned on its roof. Supplies were brought by tenders, and fresh water came from cisterns kept full by Louisiana's prodigious rains. No doubt this was a very lonely light station, but so were many others.

The Coast Guard closed up the lighthouse immediately after World War II. Abandoned and left at the mercy of high water and hurricanes for more than half a century, the rotting wooden lighthouse seems poised on the brink of extinction. However, there are those who hope to save it for posterity.

Lighthouse Digest

Louisiana's West Rigolets Lighthouse during its active years. Less land than water, the site appears far better suited to alligators and mosquitoes than to human habitation.

The station as it looks today. Most of the porch posts and many other structural details are gone, but the lantern still rises proudly from the metal roof.

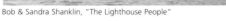

Bob & Sandra Shanklin, "The Lighthouse People"

47

FRANK'S ISLAND LIGHTHOUSE

Mississippi River Delta, Louisiana

1823

Not long after Louisiana became American soil in 1803, a fine new lighthouse was envisioned for Frank's Island. Its beacon was intended to point the way to the Mississippi River and beyond to the vast new territory opened up to settlement by the Louisiana Purchase. However, many years would pass before its beacon first guided ships to the mouth of the river. The blueprints were drawn up by Benjamin Latrobe, the noted architect who had helped complete the Capitol building, modifying the original design by William Thornton. Latrobe had also worked in England for noted lighthouse architect and engineer John Smeaton. Latrobe's design for the Frank's Island

Lighthouse proved almost as grandiose and impractical as the dreams of an overly ambitious pioneer. An ornate, Gothic Revival edifice, it included a large residence, palatial customs office, and tall light tower fashioned of brick, timber, and stone. There was even to be a marble staircase.

On other, more stable building sites, Latrobe's rather fanciful design might have been functional, but not in the swampy Mississippi Delta. The entire complex would weigh many thousands of tons and almost certainly be swallowed up by the deep Mississippi mud. No contractor—either in his right mind or otherwise—was willing to take on the project, and it languished for many years without a builder.

An exasperated Latrobe finally consented to supervise construction himself. It was a fateful—and fatal—decision. After years of sweaty struggle on the alligator-and-mosquito-infested island, Latrobe finally managed to complete his monumental lighthouse. The final courses of stone were laid in March 1820. A few days after the tower was finished it settled into the thick delta mud and collapsed. To that point the fallen lighthouse had cost the U.S. Treasury the then astounding sum of $85,000. It would also cost Latrobe his life. Not long after the tower fell, he himself collapsed and died of yellow fever. His son Henry had also died of the disease during construction.

Then into the picture stepped Winslow Lewis, the former New England sea captain who would eventually build many of America's most historic

Water surrounds the Frank's Island tower completed in 1823 by Winslow Lewis. The island itself has sunk below sea level and disappeared beneath the waves. The entrance to the Mississippi River once marked by the Frank's Island beacon now lies many miles south.

lighthouses. Lewis offered to salvage the fallen tower and replace it with a far more practical structure for the comparative bargain sum of $9,750. The government agreed to the plan, and by the spring of 1823, Lewis had completed the 82-foot masonry tower. Its lamps and reflectors, designed by Lewis himself, produced a light that could be seen from nearly 20 miles away. Having groped blindly for the Mississippi entrance for so many years, mariners now had a light to follow. Lewis and his masons did their work so well that the Frank's Island tower still stands, but it is shorter than it used to be, having sunk more than 20 feet into the mud. In fact, the island itself sank. By the 1950s it had vanished altogether, leaving the old tower standing in 10 feet of water.

Virginia Souza

The original Benjamin Latrobe design for the Frank's Island Lighthouse was grandiose and utterly impractical. Completed in 1823, the massive building soon settled into the delta mud and fell over on its side. A noted architect who had helped design the Capitol in Washington, D.C., Latrobe died of yellow fever contracted while supervising construction on Frank's Island.

PASS A L'OUTRE LIGHTHOUSE
Mississippi River Delta, Louisiana

few years after the Frank's Island Lighthouse began guiding ships into the river's Northeast Pass, this waterway became too shallow for oceangoing vessels. Most navigators then opted for the deeper waters of the once secondary Pass a l'Outre (meaning "Pass Beyond" or "the Way Out"). The light at Frank's Island, which had been established with so much trouble and expense, was discontinued, and a new light station was established at Pass a l'Outre. An iron tower, put in place by well-known lighthouse engineer Danville Leadbetter, later a Confederate general, was fitted with a revolving Fresnel lens and was ready for service late in 1855.

Even as its flashing light began to guide ships into the river and onward to New Orleans or Baton Rogue, the Pass a l'Outre Lighthouse began a slow descent into the Mississippi Delta mud. Starting out about 85 feet tall, it would lose more than a quarter of its height—shrinking in stature to just 62 feet—before the station was discontinued in 1930. Long before that time, it had lost most of its usefulness to

mariners. By the late 1880s, Pass a l'Outre had filled with huge lumps of mud, making it almost impassable to ships.

The light tower still stands, a tribute to the quality of its pre-Civil War design and construction.

Although well maintained during its years of active duty, Pass a l'Outre Lighthouse was slowly sinking into the deep Louisiana mud. The tower lost about 6 inches of its height to the mud each year.

SOUTHWEST PASS LIGHTHOUSES

Mississippi River entrance, Louisiana

1840 AND 1873

Four different lighthouses have marked the strategic Mississippi River entrance at Louisiana's Southwest Pass. Three of these towers still exist, but only the most recent of them—an oil platform-style structure completed in 1962—remains in use. Two earlier towers, dating to 1840 and 1873, remain upright, but now stand on the brink of extinction.

The first lighthouse at Southwest Pass was built by Winslow Lewis in 1832. Like many of the other lighthouses designed by Lewis, this one was short-lived. Erosion and settling soon left the station awash in the tides, and by the summer of 1837, the stone tower had fallen into the river. The high water also carried away the station's residence, forcing the keeper and his assistant to live in a squalid hut thrown together with salvaged lumber.

The entire facility was rebuilt in 1840, and again Lewis was chosen as the designer. He suggested a brick structure not at all unlike the original, and, perhaps not surprisingly, the results were once more disappointing. Shortly after the new brick tower was completed, its foundation settled into the mud, causing it to lean nearly 5 feet out of plumb. Government inspectors believed this "Leaning Tower of Southwest Pass" would soon collapse, but it did not. Although abandoned nearly a century and a half ago, the old brick tower has not yet succumbed to the tides.

Not far from the Lewis tower is the extraordinary steel skeleton structure that replaced it in 1873. Rising 128 feet above sea level, it consists of eight stout iron legs held in place by a spider's web of cross braces. The legs are supported by no less than 185 pilings painstakingly driven some 33 feet into the mud.

For nearly a century the skeleton tower at Southwest Pass remained in use, its beacon focused by a first-order Fresnel lens. This powerful light was tended by resident keepers who lived in a two-story dwelling at the base of the tower. Now rusted out, the tower is in danger of being blown over by the next Gulf hurricane that sweeps over this area.

(Above) Defying the experts, who were sure it would soon collapse, the leaning Lewis tower has remained standing for more than 160 years.

(Right) The rusting bulk of the steel skeleton tower built at Southwest Pass in 1873. Will it fall to high winds in the next hurricane?

Bob & Sandra Shanklin, "The Lighthouse People"

Bob & Sandra Shanklin, "The Lighthouse People"

SHIP SHOAL LIGHTHOUSE

South of Grand Isle, Louisiana

1859

A metal ghost from the Victorian Era rises from the waters of the Gulf of Mexico a few miles south of Grand Isle, Louisiana. Abandoned decades ago by the Coast Guard, the Ship Shoal Lighthouse was once a shining example of open water construction. Anchored to the muddy bottom by screw piles, the station's eight legs held its powerful second-order light nearly 120 feet above the waves. Keepers lived full-time in a two-story dwelling positioned safely above the water.

Built during the late 1850s at a cost of $103,000, a breathtaking sum at the time, the tower was fabricated at a distant iron foundry and then shipped to the site for assembly. The construction crews must have done their work extremely well, since the tower and its light served Gulf navigators for more than 120 years. Abandoned in 1972 and left to rust and ruin, the tower remains standing, albeit at a list of twenty degrees. The town of Berwick, Louisiana, now hopes to bring the structure ashore for use as an attraction of its community-owned Lighthouse Park.

Listing at about twenty degrees, the Ship Shoal Lighthouse still holds its lantern high above the Gulf waves. The tower may soon become part of a lighthouse attraction on shore.

Bob & Sandra Shanklin, "The Lighthouse People"

SABINE BANK LIGHTHOUSE

Near Sabine Pass, Texas

he sleepy Sabine River, forming the watery border that separates Louisiana from Texas, has never looked much like a commercial thoroughfare. To this day French-speaking fishermen work its bayous in flat-bottom boats, while egrets and herons stilt along its banks. With the arrival of the twentieth century, however, deep-water freighters began to ply the river in order to reach the docks at Port Arthur and take on loads of oil, agricultural produce, and manufactured goods. Dredged and deepened channels had made the Sabine an inland highway for oceangoing vessels, and it remains so today.

Despite the dredging, the river is an obstacle course of shoals and shallows. For eons the Sabine has dumped silt into the Gulf of Mexico, forming a formidable shoal near the river's mouth. Located about 15 miles from the mainland, the Sabine Bank lurks roughly 20 feet below the surface, waiting to rip open the hull of unwary ships. As the freighter traffic into Port Arthur grew, this dangerous shoal exacted an increasing toll of ships and sailors.

National Archives

The Sabine Bank Lighthouse under construction on shore in 1906.

To warn mariners, lighthouse officials decided to place a navigational light directly over the shoal. A foundry in Detroit assembled the tanklike iron tower and shipped it to the Gulf, where it was placed atop a massive concrete caisson. Lamps inside the station's third-order Fresnel lens were first lit on March 15, 1906.

The light's keepers were forced to remain at the isolated station for weeks or even months at a time. While on duty, they lived inside the cylindrical tower, only about 30 feet in diameter, and had little or no contact with the outside world. The station's crew survived a major hurricane in 1915, when huge waves rolled completely over the tower. Despite the pounding, they never allowed the light to go out.

An acetylene lighting system replaced the original Fresnel lens in 1923, when the light was automated, leaving the old lighthouse to stand guard over the shoal alone. Unfortunately, like many other long ago-automated lighthouses, this one has slowly deteriorated. Although it may stand for years, the rusted-out tower looks ready for the junkyard.

(Above) The Sabine Bank Lighthouse as it looked before it was automated in 1923.

(Right) The lighthouse today—a rusted-out hulk.

Lighthouse Digest

Bob & Sandra Shanklin, "The Lighthouse People"

54

SABINE PASS LIGHTHOUSE

Louisiana Point, Louisiana

1857

The Sabine River pours into the Gulf of Mexico through Sabine Pass, a relatively narrow channel located about 15 miles south of Port Arthur, Texas. On the west bank of the channel, used by ships to reach the busy, commercially vital port, is the small town of Sabine Pass, Texas. On the opposite bank, in Louisiana, is the historic lighthouse, which has guided mariners through this passage for nearly a century and a half.

Although the Sabine Pass Lighthouse was built in 1856, several years before the Civil War, the finlike concrete buttresses supporting the tower give it a surprisingly modern look. U.S. Army engineer Danville Leadbetter, who later fought for the Con-

federacy, designed several lighthouse towers along the Gulf coast, including the one at Sabine Pass. Here Leadbetter was challenged by a marshy construction site lying only about 3 feet above sea level. He knew he would have to find a way to distribute the tower's considerable weight over the unstable ground. As a solution he surrounded the tower with buttresses, which in effect gave it an extra-wide foundation. Apparently Leadbetter's experiment succeeded, since the tower has stood upright through half a dozen hurricanes and countless other powerful storms—more than 140 years' worth.

The Sabine Pass Light Station was originally a military base, placed here by order of President Martin Van Buren at the border of what was then the

One end of the keeper's residence faced a bayou used to bring in supplies by boat. Unfortunately this fine wood-frame building burned in 1974.

independent Republic of Texas. After Texas became a state in 1845, the original 20,500-acre military reservation was shrunk down to a mere forty-five acres set aside for use as a light station. However, the lighthouse itself would not be built until more than twenty years later.

That it was built at all was something of a historical accident. During much of the nineteenth century, the Sabine River was little more than a backwater. The placement of a major and, as it turned out, very expensive seamark near the river was due largely to political pressure. Texans were demanding a major federal project for their state, and Congress responded by appropriating $30,000 for the—by that time forgotten—Sabine Pass Lighthouse. Despite the availability of this relatively sizable sum as early as 1851, the difficulties of building on such a swampy site delayed progress, and the facility took almost six years to complete.

The station began operation in April 1857, but the lamps inside its third-order Fresnel lens burned for only four years before coastal fighting darkened them for the duration of the Civil War. Several sharp Civil War engagements were fought almost in the shadow of the tower. During a major Union assault on the Sabine in 1863, Confederate defenders used the lighthouse as a watchtower. The Confederates won this battle but, of course, lost the war.

Relit late in 1865, the station served until the Coast Guard discontinued it in 1952. The Coast Guard had planned to demolish the lighthouse, but as it turned out, the old tower had more friends than anyone had thought. Steve Purgley, the station's last keeper, helped form an early preservationist organization called the Sabine Pass Lighthouse Association. This group managed to block the scheduled destruction of the historic tower but was never able to raise the funds necessary to purchase the property. An effort to make the lighthouse part of a Louisiana state park eventually fizzled. Today the lighthouse is privately owned.

The current owners, however, have agreed to lease the site to the Cameron Parish Police Jury for twenty years, and the Cameron Preservation Alliance has launched a new effort to restore the lighthouse. A private, unpaved road to the lighthouse has been completed.

This recent photograph shows off the unique design of the Sabine Pass tower with its finlike buttresses. Also apparent here is the considerable damage done to the structure by weather, vandalism, and time. Notice the deteriorated condition of the walls and the missing roof on the lantern room.

GALVESTON JETTY LIGHTHOUSE

Galveston, Texas

ven before Texas won its independence from Mexico in 1836, sailors sought refuge from the stormy Gulf in the relatively calm waters of Galveston Bay. Once Texas became a state, port facilities on the bay attracted a steady stream of commercial and military sailing ships. For many years, however, the bay was closed to steam-powered vessels, which had a deeper draft and were unable to navigate the shallows at the entrance. During the late 1800s government engineers opened the door to steamers and other larger vessels by building a series of jetties to concentrate the tides and flush sand from the bottom.

Ironically the jetties themselves now became a navigational hazard. In 1894 maritime officials sought funding for a jetty lighthouse to warn approaching vessels. Congress appropriated $35,000 for the project, but war and weather would block construction for more than two decades.

Originally the Lighthouse Board envisioned a standard, shallow-water design for the station—a wooden cottage set atop iron pilings—but the deadly hurricane that swept over the area in 1900 convinced officials that such a flimsy structure could not long survive here. Among the most destructive storms in history, the hurricane and accompanying flood wrecked every building in Galveston and killed at least 6,000 people.

Alarmed by the unprecedented power of the 1900 storm, the board decided to apply twentieth-century skyscraper technology to construction of the jetty tower. The concrete superstructure would be given a framework of steel supported by heavy I-beams set on iron pilings driven deep into the stone jetty. Not surprisingly this castle-like structure could not be built within the original budget, and the board was forced to ask Congress for more

Bob & Sandra Shanklin, "The Lighthouse People"

The deteriorating Galveston Jetty Lighthouse as it appeared in 1999. The lens had been removed and placed on display at the Galveston County Historical Museum.

money. Several more hurricanes and World War I further delayed the project, and the new lighthouse was not ready for service until late in 1918.

As it turned out, the 84-foot-tall jetty lighthouse was well worth its final price of nearly $50,000. Standing up to countless gales and hurricanes, it served mariners for more than half a century. It was finally deactivated in 1972, when it was replaced by a nearby 145-foot skeleton tower.

The Galveston Jetty Lighthouse deteriorated considerably over the three decades since it was abandoned, and in 1992 it was put on the *Lighthouse Digest* Doomsday List. Realizing that the tower might not last much longer, local preservationists decided that the only way to save the weakened tower from collapse was to move it to the Galveston Island State Park. Proving just how fragile endangered lighthouses are, as this book was going to press, the Galveston Jetty Lighthouse was totally destroyed in a storm that also caused heavy damage in the Galveston area. Sadly, the lighthouse was only a matter of weeks away from being saved and moved to shore.

U.S. Coast Guard

The lighthouse during its years of active service. The concrete and steel superstructure stands on a platform supported by heavily braced steel pilings.

Steven Powell

When a recent storm swept down on the Galveston area, time ran out for the Galveston Lighthouse. This is all that remains of the once historic structure.

ENDANGERED TOWERS OF THE GREAT LAKES AND THE WEST

Ontario to California

Endangered Towers of
the Great Lakes and West

MOHAWK ISLAND LIGHTHOUSE

Near Port Maitland, Ontario

he opening of the Welland Canal across the Niagara Peninsula during the 1840s had tremendous economic significance for both Canada and the United States. By linking Lake Ontario with Lake Erie, the canal helped open up a vast expanse of the North American heartland to maritime commerce. It also generated a surge in shipping traffic at the eastern end of Lake Erie. To help guide the throng of ships passing in and out of the canal's Lake Erie entrance near Port Maitland, a key light station was established on an island about 1½ miles offshore.

Construction of the stone tower and keeper's residence on the nearly barren three-acre rock known

Wayne Sapulski

Preservationists hope to restore the 1848 Mohawk Island Lighthouse to its glory days when keepers lived here for all but a few months each year. Today this small Lake Erie island is home mostly to seagulls.

as Mohawk Island took about two years and was completed in 1848. A local farmer named John Burgess was hired as the station's first keeper at an annual salary of £65, the equivalent of about $300 U.S. This may not sound like much to us, but Burgess considered it a respectable income. He and later keepers, who no doubt earned more for their efforts, maintained the light during the lake's eight-to-nine-month navigational seasons for more than eighty years.

By the 1930s maritime officials in both Canada and the United States already had begun to automate lighthouses and remove their full-time keepers. This lengthy process would take more than half a century. In fact, a few lighthouses in western Canada still have keepers in residence. But at the Mohawk Lighthouse, the era of the resident keeper came to an end suddenly—and tragically. Toward the end of the 1932 navigational season, keeper Richard Foster and his son James were preparing to close the light station for the winter and return to their home in nearby Dunnville, Ontario. Apparently they received a radio report that their Dunnville house was on fire. Understandably distressed, the two men set off for the mainland in the midst of a blizzard. Somehow they were stranded on an ice floe and died of exposure before help could arrive. Rather than name a new keeper, the Canadian officials automated the station.

The Mohawk Island tower has walls up to 4 feet thick, and they have proven strong enough to withstand more than 150 years of the powerful storms that often roll in howling from the western end of the lake. As with many other lighthouses, however, the primary threat to this one has been what some people call progress. In 1969 the light was replaced by a floating buoy, and some years later authorities announced plans to demolish the historic tower. Canadian preservationists rushed to the defense of the lighthouse and managed to save it.

Unfortunately little has been done since to restore the building. Its hollow walls lie open to the weather and are a frequent target of vandals. Help is on the way, however. The Mohawk Lighthouse Preservation Association in Lowbanks, Ontario, is raising money for an ambitious restoration effort—to be supported entirely with private funding and without government assistance.

GREEN ISLAND (LAKE ERIE) LIGHTHOUSE

North of Port Clinton, Ohio

1855

Even many lighthouse experts have never heard of the Green Island Light Station, once a key navigational aid in western Lake Erie. Hidden behind a screen of tall deciduous trees, the lighthouse has all but vanished from time and memory. Abandoned by the Coast Guard in 1939 and gutted by fire some decades later, the stone tower and residence now seem less man-made than a natural part of the island.

Green Island, located about 15 miles northwest of Sandusky, Ohio, was long noted for its geology. A rare specimen mineral called strontianite was once found there. Collectors eventually exhausted the supply of strontianite, a form of crystallized celestite, but the island still had plenty of glitter. Its sparkle came from the bottle-green Fresnel lens atop the island's limestone lighthouse tower. Established in 1855, the Green Island Light Station guided ships through an archipelago of nearly two dozen small islands cluttering southwestern Lake Erie.

The island's first lighthouse served for only eight years before it was destroyed in a disastrous fire on

National Archives

The first Green Island Lighthouse, built in 1855 and destroyed by fire in 1863. The keeper and his family were saved, but not their possessions.

Completed in 1865, this attractive stone lighthouse was home to Green Island keepers and their families for more than sixty years.

December 31, 1963. This New Year's Eve fire broke out in the midst of a tremendous blizzard that had swept in earlier in the day, dropping the temperature from an almost balmy sixty degrees Fahrenheit to a bone-freezing twenty-five degrees below zero. The keeper, Colonel Charles F. Drake, and his family had gathered in the sitting room to celebrate the approach of the New Year when a loud crackling sound alerted them to danger. Colonel Drake rushed to the light tower and found the entire upper portion in flames.

The keeper tried in vain to fight the fire with dampened clothing and buckets of water carried from the lake by his wife and daughter. Soon the Drake family was forced to retreat with the few possessions they managed to pull from the blaze. At considerable risk to life and limb, a party of rescuers from a nearby island fought their way across the icy lake to reach the stricken lighthouse on New Year's Day. There they found the keeper and his family huddled in the station outhouse, shielding themselves from the cold with a singed feather mattress.

The Lighthouse Board ordered the burned-out lighthouse to be pulled down and replaced by a handsome, two-story limestone keeper's residence and attached light tower. Completed in 1865, just at the end of the Civil War, the structure somewhat resembled a modest midwestern church with a squared-off bell tower. In this case, however, instead of a bell, the tower held aloft a bright Fresnel lens.

Keepers and their families lived comfortably at the new station for more than sixty years. For schooling, children made daily trips to the mainland, by dogsled in winter and by water the rest of the year. Chickens, cows, and other livestock had the run of the island, and one keeper even had a splendid team of Italian greyhounds. This bucolic lifestyle continued until 1926, when the Lighthouse Service boarded up the residence and automated the beacon.

The light remained active until 1939 when a new Green Island Light was installed in a utilitarian iron tower. After that, the old stone lighthouse began to slowly deteriorate. Its ruin accelerated considerably when a fire started by a party of trespassing vandals gutted the building. All that remains today is its limestone shell.

Ruined in a fire started by vandals, the station appears to be returning to nature. Its windows now open only onto emptiness.

TURTLE ISLAND LIGHTHOUSE

Near Toledo, Ohio

The ancient square tower of the Turtle Island Lighthouse is a familiar sight to boaters on Maumee Bay near Toledo, Ohio. To many it may seem more of an apparition, a ghost tower, than a true brick structure built by human hands, because each time they look the tower seems to have crumbled a bit more and sunk a little closer to the waters it once so boldly marked. Their eyes do not deceive them. Under siege by overgrown shrubs, scrubby trees, and the encroaching waters of Lake Erie itself, the tower is going fast, and it will disappear altogether unless something is done to save it—and soon.

For more than seventy years freighters and other vessels plying the western reaches of Lake Erie counted on the bright beacon of the Turtle Island Lighthouse to point the way to Toledo. Established in 1832, the station served until about 1904, when the Toledo Harbor Light took over the task of guiding ships into port. Abandoned by the government, the historic lighthouse eventually fell victim to wind, weather, and vandals, who carried away bricks, tim-

The Turtle Island Lighthouse in better days. Notice the keeper and his family standing in front of the tower. The brick retaining wall in the foreground was built to hold back the waters of the lake.

bers, nails, and anything that could be loaded into a small boat. Eventually the roof and walls of the two-story dwelling caved in, leaving only the sturdy, reinforced tower as a monument to the station's long term of service.

Turtle Island and its lighthouse share a rich history. The island was named for Little Turtle, a Miami tribal chieftain who brought his people to the shores of Lake Erie during the summer. It is said the Indians regularly visited the island to gather the eggs of seagulls that nested there by the hundreds.

During the late 1700s, a period of almost constant conflict along the frontier, the British seized the island and built a log fort there. They hoped the fort would help them cut off supplies to American forces under General Anthony Wade, who was trying to push back an Indian army and solidify U.S. territo-

Bob & Sandra Shanklin, "The Lighthouse People"

rial claims in the Midwest. Despite the fort, the necessary supplies reached General Wade, who won a key victory at the Battle of Fallen Timbers in 1794.

The surge of commercial shipping on the Great Lakes during the early nineteenth century made it necessary to mark key ports, such as the one at Toledo, with navigational lights. In 1831 Congress appropriated $5,000 for construction of a lighthouse on Turtle Island, strategically located near the entrance to the Toledo harbor. Another $2,000 was set aside to shore up the island, which even then was shrinking.

It may be that the slow sinking of the island undermined the 1930s lighthouse. After thirty years of service, it was found to be in a severe state of disrepair, so much so that the entire structure had to be torn down and rebuilt. The handsome building that replaced it was constructed of high-quality Milwaukee brick and completed shortly after the Civil War. A two-and-a-half-story dwelling with attached tower, the new lighthouse was considered among the finest navigational facilities on the Great Lakes. A fourth-order light beamed out over the lake from atop the tower.

Although the lighthouse remained sound for decades, the island itself continued to shrink. Throughout the late 1800s engineers struggled to hold back the lake. Pilings, landfill, and even a concrete retaining wall only delayed the inevitable. Originally more than seven acres, the island has today dwindled to a mere scrap of gravelly soil.

In recent years concerned citizens and preservation groups in the Toledo area have made plans to shore up what remains of the island. They also hope to restore the old tower or, at least, keep it from falling even further into ruin. But so far nothing definitive has been done. The last days of the Turtle Island tower may be approaching, and if it is finally carried away by time or the waters of the lake, much valuable history will disappear along with it.

The station today. Only the tower remains; its lantern room long ago vanished. Turtle Island continues to shrink, and, as can be seen here, the waters of Lake Erie now lap rocks only a few feet from the base of the tower.

BOIS BLANC LIGHTHOUSE
Near Amhurstburg, Ontario

1836

Near the point where the Detroit River, fed by the overflowing waters of the upper lakes, empties into Lake Erie, is an island given the name Bois Blanc ("White Woods") by early French explorers. Their tongues twisted by the French words, local English-speaking people came to call the place "Boblo." It was on Bois Blanc or Boblo Island that the Canadian government built a lighthouse in 1836 to mark the Lake Erie entrance to the river.

Contractors gave the station a sturdy 40-foot stone tower with walls 5-feet thick at the base. The beacon shining from atop the tower was produced

Institute for Great Lakes Research

Shown here in its heyday, the Bois Blanc Lighthouse marked the Lake Erie entrance to the Detroit River.

For many years a small automated light shined from the old Bois Blanc (Boblo Island) tower.

The Bois Blanc tower is no longer used as a navigational marker.

by a dozen 16-inch reflectors. The keeper's cottage, also made of stone, measured approximately 20 feet by 30 feet. Both structures were built using Lake Erie limestone, apparently brought to the area as ballast in ships.

The station's first keeper, a man named James Hacket, was likely among the few Canadian government employees ever to get his job in exchange for a dog. It is said the governor of Upper Canada happened to be in Amhurstburg when the lighthouse was completed. For some reason the governor thought the Hacket family mutt an especially fine animal and offered to buy it. The Hackets refused to sell but instead agreed to give up their dog in exchange for the job as keeper at the new lighthouse.

James Hacket was made the official keeper, but it was his wife who actually took care of the light and kept it fueled with whale oil. Most of the time James Hacket was on the water earning additional income as a lake pilot.

Around the turn of the twentieth century, investors built an amusement park on Boblo Island. It was a favorite destination for Detroit families on summer afternoons. The old amusement park is gone now, but the tower of the neighboring lighthouse still stands. The lantern room and lighting apparatus disappeared many years ago, as did the stone keeper's dwelling. In time the crumbling tower itself may vanish.

CHARITY ISLAND LIGHTHOUSE

Saginaw Bay, Michigan

1859

Near the mouth of Michigan's famed Saginaw Bay lies a 322-acre island named Big Charity. A mature maple forest cloaks the island's highlands. Rare wildflowers adorn its open fields. Sparkling white dunes line its beaches. It even has its own emerald lake—a lake on an island in the middle of a lake. Big Charity Island is a window on the past, a throwback to the time when all the lower Great Lakes were once vast wilderness. Now only a few tiny, widely scattered patches of that wilderness remain, and they are threatened.

Big Charity Island harbors another sort of throwback, a decaying lighthouse in danger of disappearing forever. Built here not long before the Civil War, the historic structure is almost a century and a half old. The station was abandoned by the government in 1939, and since that time, its buildings have been left more or less at the mercy of the elements. The once bright lantern atop the brick tower has been dark for almost a lifetime. The station residence stands empty and in ruins, almost on the point of collapse.

Long before the first Europeans reached the heart of the continent, Native American canoes regularly landed on the island, known to be rich in chert, a flinty material used for making tools. Later the island became a refuge for fishermen caught in the sudden storms that often savage Saginaw Bay. The fishermen were so thankful for the shelter that they believed the island must have been placed by God as an act of charity. Thus the island got its name.

Located some 7 miles offshore, about midway between Point Lookout to the northwest and Sand Point to the south, the island also provided a convenient natural marker for sailors navigating the commercially strategic bay. During the late 1850s the Lighthouse Board decided to make the island even more useful by building a lighthouse there. By 1857 the brick tower and wooden dwelling had been completed at a cost to the U.S. Treasury of $4,819.

For more than forty years, resident keepers and their assistants lived on the island, climbing its tower each night to maintain the light. The Charity Island residence was boarded up after 1900, when an automated acetylene lamp was placed in the tower, eliminating the need for full-time keepers. For four decades the lighthouse continued its vigil alone. Then, in 1939, a new light was established at Gravelly Shoal about a mile away, and the Big Charity Light was snuffed out.

The federal property on the island was eventually sold off to private interests. Recognizing its scenic and historic attractions, the owners now hope to

The Charity Island Lighthouse tower still stands tall, but its duplex residence has seen better days.

develop the island. As part of the development plan, the old lighthouse is to be at least partially restored. The tower remains in reasonably good condition and still has its lantern, minus any sort of lighting device. Unfortunately the old residence may be beyond help. Generations of island campers have pulled away the board siding for use in campfires. The metal roof is still sound, but otherwise little is left but a skeleton.

WAUGOSHANCE LIGHTHOUSE
West of Mackinaw City, Michigan

1851

Ships are at home in open water, but when they approach land, their captains grow fearful, and for good reason. Large vessels may survive the pounding of waves as tall as a tenstory building, but whenever they become trapped in the shallows or their hulls strike something solid, such as a reef, the result is almost invariably disaster. This is one reason the Great Lakes are so dangerous. Constricted by their long rocky shorelines, they are strewn with shoals and sandbanks. Naturally enough, the most dangerous places are the narrows that link them, such as the treacherous Straits of Mackinac between Lakes Michigan and Huron. During the early 1800s, as lake commerce grew, more and more ships passed through the straits, carrying passengers, minerals, coal, lumber, and manufactured goods. More than a few never reached their destinations.

National Archives

Protected from waves and winter ice by walls of concrete and steel, the Waugoshance Lighthouse was kept shipshape during its more than fifty years of service. The station was decommissioned in 1912 after a nearby light made it redundant.

To the west of Mackinaw City, Waugoshance Point extends threateningly into Lake Michigan. A maze of rocks, reefs, and small islands extends more than 8 miles beyond the point. A sailor lost here in a storm or fog may never see home again. During the 1830s a lightship known as the *Louis McLane* was anchored here to help pilots pick their way through this deadly obstacle course. But not until midcentury was a permanent light station established off the point.

Completed in 1851, the Waugoshance Lighthouse was built offshore atop a crib of wood and stone. This was the first Great Lakes lighthouse to be erected on a crib, but engineers must have had considerable faith in the technique. They gave the station a massive 76-foot tower with walls 5-feet thick. At the top was a polygonal birdcage lantern, fitted with a state-of-the-art Fresnel lens—among the first to serve on the lakes.

By 1865 Lake Michigan's crushing winter ice had ground away much of the original crib. To save the lighthouse, the government surrounded it with a heavy coffer dam, creating the artificial shoal on which the tower stands today. Even so, the lighthouse remained under assault by weather and ice. The soft bricks of the tower and residence began to crumble, and in 1883 they were encased in a shell of steel boilerplate, painted with red and white horizontal bands for better visibility. At about the same time, the station's fog bell was replaced by a steam whistle. Captains and their pilots tended to confuse the bell with those of passing ships, and at least one serious wreck—that of the schooner *Flying Mist* in 1881—was blamed on the confusion.

Over the years the Waugoshance Lighthouse helped save countless other vessels from a fate similar to that of *Flying Mist*. Ironically it may now be impossible to save the old light station itself. Decommissioned in 1912 after it was made obsolete by the nearby White Shoals Light, it has stood up to nearly ninety years of harsh winter storms, neglect, vandalism, and other abuse. Navy bombers have used the tower for target practice, causing fires that have gutted the interior of the tower and dwelling. Vandals and souvenir hunters have made off with fittings, the copper sheeting that covered the lantern room, and even the iron spiral staircase that generations of keepers climbed in order to tend the Waugoshance Light.

As long ago as 1983, the Coast Guard recommended the tower be pulled down and removed as a safety hazard, but this has not yet been done. The tower still stands, and from a distance it looks much like a tombstone rising out of the lake. Perhaps it makes a fitting monument to the thousands of sailors and passengers who have lost their lives in the lakes. The comparison to a gravestone is made all the more fitting by the station's ghostly reputation. Some say the tower is haunted by the spirit of a keeper who drowned here during the nineteenth century.

Lighthouse Digest

Nine decades of abuse and neglect have left little of the Waugoshance Light Station intact. Gutted in a fire set by an errant Navy missile, the tower still stands. The crumbling structure reminds some of a tombstone—appropriately enough, since it is supposedly haunted.

SOUTH FOX ISLAND LIGHTHOUSE

Northeast of Cat Head Point, Michigan

1867

With its lush greenery and spectacular beaches, South Fox Island may remind some visitors of paradise. But for navigators trying to thread their way through the maze of obstacles in northern Lake Michigan, it has a somewhat more sinister reputation. The island's sweeping arc cuts like a saber across the lake's crowded shipping lanes. More than a few hapless mariners have made an unexpected and disastrous landfall on the sands of the island.

The government established a light station here in 1867. Built for approximately $18,000, it consisted of a two-story brick residence with an attached tower. Square and 45-feet tall, the tower held aloft a bull's-eye Fresnel lens, which rotated on ball bearings.

To give the light a boost and make it visible from a greater distance, the Coast Guard erected a much taller steel skeleton tower on the island in 1934. The tower had originally stood on Georgia's Sapelo Island, but was dismantled, shipped to Michigan, and reassembled on South Fox Island.

The South Fox Island Light Station was deactivated decades ago. Although both towers and other key structures still stand, they need extensive restoration and are considered endangered. Now owned by the state of Michigan, the property may soon be sold to a private developer, placing the fate of the historic light station in doubt.

An aerial view of South Fox Island Light Station. Note the two towers. The square brick tower on the left was completed in 1867, just two years after the Civil War. The iron skeleton tower on the right was moved here from Georgia's Sapelo Island in 1934.

POVERTY ISLAND LIGHTHOUSE

Near Fairport, Upper Peninsula, Michigan

1874

From the Michigan Upper Peninsula a long finger of land points into Lake Michigan, extending southwestward to within a few dozen miles of Wisconsin's Door Peninsula. If the two peninsulas touched, they would close off Green Bay, making it a separate lake of considerable size. The heavily traveled passage between the lake and the bay is strewn with islands and threatening rocks. This has always been a dangerous place for ships. To help them clear the passage safely, federal authorities established an important light station on Poverty Island, just south of Fairport, Michigan.

Completed in 1874, the station's primary building consisted of a brick, stone, and wood residence with an attached 60-foot tower. Originally the light was produced by a fourth-order Fresnel lens with a focal plane about 80 feet above the water; the elevation of the site gives the tower a boost of about 20 feet. Automated since 1957, the station now employs a 300 mm aeromarine beacon. When the automated light was installed, the lantern room was removed from the tower.

No Coast Guard keepers have lived here on a regular basis since the 1950s. Like other abandoned or orphaned lighthouses, the absence of human occupants has been hard on the century-and-a-quarter-old building. Because the tower remains in use, it has been somewhat better cared for than the residence.

The Poverty Island Lighthouse and its decapitated tower. Deactivated in 1976, the light was returned to service in 1982. The automated beacon still guides mariners.

Lighthouse Digest

LONG TAIL POINT LIGHTHOUSE

Near Suamico, Wisconsin

1849

ot far from the bustling Wisconsin port city of Green Bay, a long, low, and narrow point of land extends for several miles southeastward into the cold blue-green waters of the bay for which the port is named. On a map the peninsula resembles the flowing tail of a horse, and no doubt that is why it came to be called Long Tail Point. Once there were houses and small farms on the point. Now all these are gone. Today the only remaining man-made structure is a ruin known to locals as "the Old Stone Tower."

The tower has a fragile look, as if it might tumble down in the next strong wind. In fact, it is a tough survivor. Built in 1849 as a light tower intended to guide vessels through the lower reaches of Green Bay,

Bob & Sandra Shanklin, "The Lighthouse People"

it was permanently abandoned just twelve years later when erosion undercut its foundation. Originally 65 feet tall, the 5-foot-thick walls of the tower had been constructed with the cheapest material available—stones gathered from surrounding fields and from the shoreline of the bay. It was expected to collapse soon after it was abandoned in favor of a nearby structure built with far more conventional materials—high-quality lumber and brick. However, it proved far more durable than anyone imagined. It outlasted not only its replacement, but a third lighthouse as well, and even defied an attempt to tear it down.

A combination tower and dwelling, the second Long Tail Point Lighthouse stood for more than seventy-five years. Although its light was relocated to a nearby open water tower in 1898, it remained in use as a residence for keepers until the station was automated during the 1930s. It was later sold to a local man for use as a private house, with the understanding that he move it to another site. During a midwinter attempt to pull the heavy building across the frozen bay, it broke through the ice and was crushed. A few of its timbers were salvaged and later used in construction of a farm silo. The offshore tower was destroyed when a sharp winter gale washed it off its pilings in 1973.

The Old Stone Tower might well have fallen during the 1970s as well. Considered an eyesore by the government, it was to be torn down. Removing the heavy stones took far more effort than expected, however, and the defiant tower was left in place to the delight of all who respect history and love lighthouses.

Defying the predictions of experts who thought it sure to fall more than 150 years ago, the original Long Tail Point tower still stands.

The second of three Long Tail Point Lighthouses, this combination residence and tower was home to keepers from 1859 until the station was automated in 1936.

GREEN ISLAND (LAKE MICHIGAN) LIGHTHOUSE

Near Marinette, Wisconsin

During the latter half of the nineteenth century and into the early twentieth, there was an active Green Island Lighthouse in both Lake Erie and Lake Michigan. One helped mariners weave their way through a string of small islands just north of Sandusky, Ohio, while the other guided freighters through the chilly waters of Wisconsin's Green Bay. Ironically both these Great Lakes lighthouses now lie in ruins, the victims of fire and neglect.

Located just to the east of Marinette, Wisconsin, the westernmost of the two Green Island Lighthouses marked the midpoint of heavily trafficked Green Bay. For much of the station's more than half century of service, it was kept by members of a single family. During the late 1860s, career Lighthouse Service man Samuel Drew became the keeper here and made of the isolated island station a comfortable home for his wife and five children. Food, supplies, and medicines were brought from the mainland by means of a small sailboat, which could not be used in all weather. Unfortunately a storm prevented Drew from reaching the mainland when his youngest daughter, the three-month-old Anna, fell ill during the fall of 1869. She died for lack of medical treatment and was buried on the island.

Two years after Anna's death, the Drew family witnessed one of the nation's worst natural disasters. During the hot, dry summer of 1871, the great Pestigo fire consumed entire forests on the mainland and gobbled up one small town after another. Smoke from the fire darkened the sky for days, leading the Drews to wonder if the world was coming to an end. Because of the darkness, Drew kept the station light burning day and night.

The keeper's oldest son, Frank Drew, grew up on Green Island and eventually took over as keeper of the station himself. As a youth Frank Drew had served on tugs, fishing boats, and freighters, and in time he became a lake pilot and captain of his own vessel. When the job as assistant keeper at Green Island came open, Drew eagerly accepted the position. He remained on the island for seventeen years, until he retired from the Lighthouse Service in 1919. The Coast Guard eventually honored Frank Drew by naming one of its cutters after him.

(Left) The Green Island Light Station during its active years. (Right) Abandoned during the 1930s, the Green Island Light Station fell into ruin. Like its namesake in Lake Erie, this historic stone lighthouse was burned by vandals. Now all that remains is a hollow stone shell.

GRAND ISLAND EAST CHANNEL LIGHTHOUSE
Near Munising, Michigan

1867

One of Michigan's most recognizable landmarks is in danger of collapse. For generations boaters going in and out of Munising on the shore of Michigan's Upper Peninsula have taken pleasure in the familiar sight of the long-ago abandoned Grand Island East Channel Lighthouse. Although the building was once a shipshape, government light station, it now resembles something more like a crudely built country church.

The stone and wood combination tower and keeper's residence was built in 1867 to mark a key channel linking the port at Munising to the open waters of Lake Superior. Among several light stations established on the lake after the opening of the

Soo Locks in 1855, it served as a significant aid to navigation for more than forty years. The station was decommissioned in 1913, however, after the construction of a set of more useful range lights at nearby Grand Island Harbor. Since that time the structure has been left largely at the mercy of the elements, and barely a fleck of paint can be found on its walls.

Maintenance of the lighthouse has not been a government responsibility for more than eighty-five years. In 1915 a forty-four-acre island tract was sold, along with the lighthouse, to a group of twenty private owners. The land was distributed in subdivided parcels to the owners, with each retaining part ownership of the lighthouse. Over the years the

Lighthouse Digest

During almost half a century of active service, the Grand Island East Channel Light Station was well maintained by its U.S. Lighthouse Service keepers.

The Grand Island East Channel Lighthouse now stands hard by the shore of Lake Superior, its foundation threatened by encroaching water. Some preservationists would like to see the structure completely restored. Most local boaters and tourists, however, find the building's dilapidated appearance appealing and romantic.

This photograph shows what time and neglect have done to the historic lighthouse.

Chris Case

parcels have been combined, resold, and passed on to relatives, with the result that it is no longer clear just who owns the lighthouse.

From time to time parcel owners and other private interests have made attempts to preserve the historic structure. In 1984 enough money was raised to enclose the windows and doors and replace the rotten roof. However, the lighthouse now faces a threat even more menacing than the harsh Upper Peninsula weather—the lake itself. Erosion has brought Lake Superior's churning waters to within a few feet of the foundation. In fact, the water has

already undercut part of the foundation and appears to be working its away around to the rear. In time, if the building doesn't fall down first, it will be standing on an island.

Midwestern preservationists and other lighthouse friends hope to save this severely endangered eighteenth-century treasure. Unfortunately meaningful restoration work will take far more money than is currently available. The American Lighthouse Foundation has provided a matching grant to provide seed money for the effort.

GRANITE ISLAND LIGHTHOUSE

North of Marquette, Michigan

1869

The hard stone walls of the Granite Island Lighthouse have withstood more than 130 of Lake Superior's stormy winters. Completed in 1869, a few years after the Civil War, the combination residence and tower is made of tough stuff—appropriately enough, granite. Nonetheless, this Lighthouse Service veteran · shows its age all too clearly. Its joints are cracking, its windows are boarded up, its ceiling has caved in, and everywhere its faded paint is peeling. Automated and more or less abandoned in 1939 when the Coast Guard took charge of this and other U.S. lighthouses, the station has been watched over only by gulls for more than sixty years.

Nearly a dozen miles from shore in a lake notorious for its sudden deadly squalls, Granite Island was always considered a lonely outpost. Keepers and their assistants had to live on the nearly barren two-and-a-half-acre island full-time in order to maintain the light and fog signal here. They were allowed to leave only during the winter, when the lake froze over and navigation was impossible.

Like its neighboring light on Huron Island, several dozen miles to the northwest, the Granite Island Lighthouse guarded a key navigation obstacle—the rocky island itself. After the discovery of copper and iron ore on the Michigan Upper Peninsula during the mid-1800s, commercial shipping in Lake Superior increased dramatically. Vessels moving along the south side of the lake or visiting the busy port of Marquette were threatened by a jagged outcropping of granite known to local Indians as Na-Be-Quon, or Canoe with a Hump. By the spring of 1869, a bright beacon, focused by a fourth-order Fresnel lens, was warning mariners away from Na-Be-Quon, which was later renamed Granite Island.

Both lighthouses served generations of lake navigators, and both are now endangered (see page 80 for information on the Huron Island Lighthouse). The government recently put Granite Island and its lighthouse up for sale. The winning bid, submitted by a private individual, amounted to just over $86,000. The new owner, a lifelong Michigan resident, plans to restore the lighthouse and open it for tours.

Don Nelson

The Granite Island Lighthouse crowns a barren two-and-a-half-acre rock, once a key threat to navigation. Today most ships keep well away from the island, still marked by a small automated light.

HURON ISLAND LIGHTHOUSE

Lake Superior, northwest of Big Bay, Michigan

1868

Early on the morning of May 29, 1860, a heavy blanket of fog lay over Lake Superior as the sidewheel steamer *Arctic* plowed through nearly still waters a few miles off the shore of Michigan's Upper Peninsula. The *Arctic*'s captain, aware of the threat represented by the scatter of rocks and islets known as the Huron Islands, had his vessel running at reduced speed until he was sure he had cleared these dangerous obstacles. Believing he had put the Hurons behind him, the captain gave the order to change course and put on more steam. Minutes later the wooden hull of the *Arctic* was torn open by rock just off the westernmost island in the Huron chain.

The story of this maritime disaster ends more happily than most. Although the *Arctic* was left a hopeless wreck, passengers, crew, baggage, and cargo were all salvaged and deposited safely on the island. Even the herd of cattle that happened to be on board made it onto the island without the loss of a head. Although marooned on the island for a couple days, the castaways—both human and bovine—were eventually rescued by a passing steamer.

To prevent similar accidents and mark the commercially important route to the Keweenaw Peninsula, the Lighthouse Board decided to place a navigational station in the Hurons. However, the Civil war delayed construction, and the lighthouse was not completed and in operation until 1868. The granite and mortar tower was only 39 feet tall, but since it stood on a high rock, its light shined out over the lake from a point nearly 200 feet above the water. The powerful beacon was focused by a Fresnel lens of a type made especially for use in the Great Lakes and slightly smaller than a standard third-order coastal lens.

For more than a century the light guided mariners through the Hurons. Despite the presence of the light, however, not every vessel was able to clear the islands safely. Among those that foundered on the rocks here were the schooner *Cambridge* (1873), the schooner *Southwest* (1898), the *Iosco* and its barge *Olive-Jeanette* (1905), the *George Nester* (1909), which sank with all seven hands, and countless lesser craft.

The need for guidance here is still recognized, and to this day, the passage remains lighted. An automated light now serves the station, its batteries recharged by solar panels. The original Huron Station lens remained in use until 1972, when the automated system was installed. At that time the last full-time keepers and staff departed, leaving the tower, residence, and other station buildings to the ravages of the weather.

Nowadays the Huron Islands are managed by the U.S. Fish and Wildlife Service as part of the Seney Wildlife Refuge. Perhaps correctly, the service sees its primary responsibility here as protection of the environmentally sensitive islands and not the maintenance of historic structures. Over the years the harsh climate has taken its toll on the station buildings, but the lighthouse is not without its friends. A group of concerned citizens—the Huron Island Lighthouse Preservation Association—has been formed to save the historic light station, and has already completed many repairs.

The attractive stone Huron Island Lighthouse tower and residence appear in relatively good shape. However, this exterior view does not show the damage caused by the building's leaky roof. Fortunately the roof was recently repaired.

GULL ROCK LIGHTHOUSE

Lake Superior, off Keweenaw Peninsula, Michigan

1867

Located in the open waters of Lake Superior nearly 2 miles off the tip of Michigan's Keweenaw Peninsula, Gull Rock has always served as a roost for birds. During the summer months, when there are plenty of small fish and other food resources in the area, thousands of gulls gather daily on the rock—hence the name. In 1867, however, the rock's avian residents had to make way for a rather large newcomer, a lighthouse that took up nearly half the small island's limited space.

After the Civil War, shipping traffic on the Great Lakes increased dramatically, spurring additional lighthouse construction. On stormy Lake Superior, a light station was established on Gull Rock to guide vessels safely around the Keweenaw Peninsula, which jutted 100 miles or more out into the lake. From 1867 until the station was automated decades ago, keepers had to live at the station full-time to maintain the light.

Some keepers who served at Gull Rock considered it to be among the loneliest light stations in America. Certainly it was among the most isolated. The restless waters of the lake encroached on the station from all sides. There was no arable ground for growing vegetables, so all food supplies had to be brought in from the mainland. Usually keepers and their families (who often lived with them) were able to leave the station during the winter months when the lakes were iced over and not navigable.

Little has been done to protect the lighthouse in recent years. Annually beleaguered by ice and pounded by the lake's prodigious summer storms, the building may eventually collapse. Gull Rock and its weathered lighthouse are off-limits to the public. The automated light remains operational.

Often under assault by summer storms and winter ice, Gull Rock Lighthouse still clings to its open-water rock in Lake Superior. Built in 1867, the tower and residence are in disrepair, but the light remains operational. Long ago automated, the beacon is powered by batteries recharged daily by the solar panels seen here at the right side of the tower.

FOURTEEN MILE POINT LIGHTHOUSE

Near Ontanogon, Michigan

1894

L island's limited space.

After the Civil War, shipping traffic on the Great Lakes increased dramatically, spurring additional lighthouse construction. On stormy Lake Superior, a light station was established on Gull Rock to guide vessels safely around the Keweenaw Peninsula, which jutted 100 miles or more out into the lake. From 1867 until the station was automated decades ago, keepers had to live at the station full-time to maintain the light.

Some keepers who served at Gull Rock considered it to be among the loneliest light stations in America. Certainly it was among the most isolated. The restless waters of the lake encroached on the station from all sides. There was no arable ground for growing vegetables, so all food supplies had to be brought in from the mainland. Usually keepers and their families (who often lived with them) were able to leave the station during the winter months when the lakes were iced over and not navigable.

Little has been done to protect the lighthouse in recent years. Annually beleaguered by ice and pounded by the lake's prodigious summer storms, the building may eventually collapse. Gull Rock and its weathered lighthouse are off-limits to the public. The automated light remains operational.

ocated on a wild and remote stretch of Lake Supe-

The hollow walls of the burned-out lighthouse suggest its former magnificence.

A vintage photograph of Michigan's Fourteen Mile Lighthouse—more impressive than the town halls of many midwestern communities. The group in the foreground may include keepers, assistants, and their families.

OUTER ISLAND LIGHTHOUSE

Apostle Islands National Lakeshore, Wisconsin

1874

One of several light stations established during the 1800s to guide vessels around and through the mazelike Apostle Islands, the Outer Island Lighthouse went into service in 1874. Positioned on top of a 40-foot, red-clay bluff, the station's tall, 90-foot brick tower gave the beacon exceptional range. Outer Island Light could be seen by ships far out in Lake Superior.

Today the same bluff that boosted the elevation of the tower and made its light more effective may now destroy the old lighthouse. The clay is eroding at an alarming rate, as much as a foot a year, and the edge of the cliff now lies less than 60 feet from the foundation of the tower. The nearby fog signal building stands less than 50 feet from the edge. The margin of safety grows smaller with each passing year, and long before the precipice reaches the station's historic buildings, something will have to be done to protect them. Otherwise they will be lost.

Little or no thought was give to erosion when the lighthouse was built during the 1870s. The prime consideration then was the safety of the crews and cargoes of ore freighters plying the waters of Lake Superior in ever greater numbers. The powerful Outer Island beacon and fog signal provided a key link in the chain of navigational markers guiding ships from Duluth to the locks at Sault Ste. Marie.

Originally the flashing light was focused by a rotating third-order Fresnel lens with six bull's-eye panels. The prismatic lens was removed and replaced by a modern aeromarine beacon when the station was fully automated in 1961. Early on, the fog signal building held a locomotive steam whistle, but that was replaced by a compressed air diaphonic horn in 1925.

Held in trust by the National Park Service, the Outer Island Lighthouse is not among the most threatened of America's light stations, but it is endangered by erosion. Its exceptional beauty and historic qualities make its loss unthinkable.

Michael Shedlock

The lovely whitewashed brick tower of the Outer Island Lighthouse stands less than 60 feet from the edge of a rapidly eroding bluff. This attractive structure is one of several fine lighthouses located in Wisconsin's Apostle Islands National Lakeshore.

RASPBERRY ISLAND LIGHTHOUSE

Apostle Islands National Lakeshore, Wisconsin

1863

Like its neighbor on the Apostles' Outer Island, the Raspberry Island Lighthouse is threatened by erosion. The clay bluff in front of the historic structure is washing away at a rate of up to a foot a year, and in places the cliff is less than 30 feet away from the tower and residence. Fortunately for those who love lighthouses and are anxious to see them preserved, the Raspberry Island and Outer Island Lighthouses are now watched over by the U.S. Park Service and maintained as popular attractions of the Apostle Islands National Lakeshore. It is hard to imagine that the government will allow either of these fine structures to be lost. Even so, both are now endangered, and it is not clear what will be done to save them. A retaining wall built along the Raspberry Island bluffs in 1985 has slowed, but not stopped, the erosion.

The Raspberry Island Lighthouse is the most frequently visited of the six light stations located within the national lakeshore. Living history performances are conducted here during the summer months when tour boats make regular stops at the station. The main building, a handsome combination residence and tower, contains a fascinating museum.

Equipped with a relatively modest fifth-order Fresnel lens—now removed and on display in a museum on Madeline Island—the Rasperry Island Station was never considered the most important or prominent of the Apostles' lighthouses. Its task was to mark the key west channel that traversed the island maze and provided a shortcut for vessels attempting to avoid the longer and stormier route around the chain. Even so, visitors today may feel they've reached the very heart of the American lighthouse heritage.

A popular summertime attraction, the Raspberry Island Lighthouse in the Apostle Islands National Lakeshore is under threat by erosion. Established in 1863, the station guided vessels into a key navigable channel that cut through the Apostles. The name was given to the chain by early missionaries who thought there were twelve islands. Actually there are more than twenty.

MINNESOTA POINT LIGHTHOUSE

Near Duluth, Minnesota

1858

Only a broken and crumbling brick tower marks the spot where the Minnesota Point Lighthouse once stood. Established in 1858, the light station guided freighters in and out of Duluth's busy industrial harbor for twenty years. By 1878, however, sand and silt had shifted the channel southward, rendering the lighthouse all but useless. The lens and other equipment were removed and placed in a tower at the end of a lengthy harbor pier. That lighthouse still stands, but all that remains of the Minnesota Point Station are its shattered ruins.

Bob & Sandra Shanklin, "The Lighthouse People"

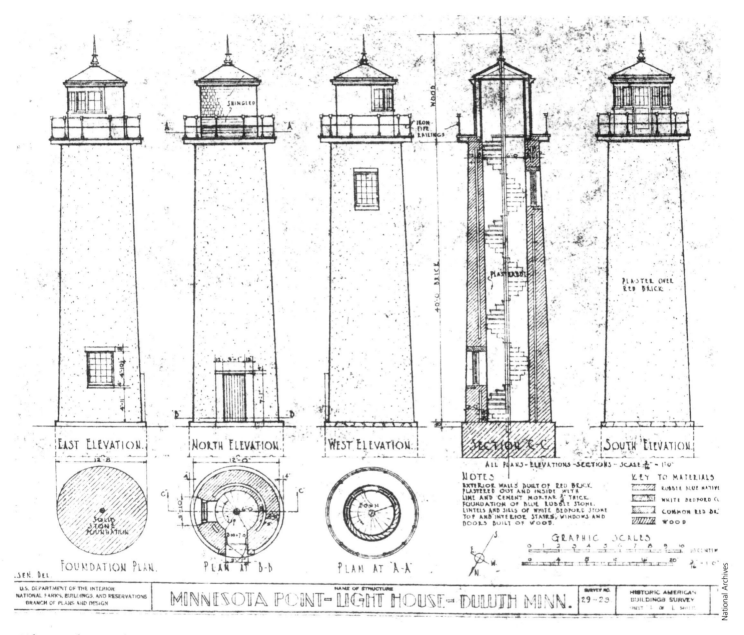

EAST ELEVATION.

NORTH ELEVATION.

WEST ELEVATION.

SECTION C-C

SOUTH ELEVATION

FOUNDATION PLAN.

PLAN AT B-B

PLAN AT A-A

ALL PLANS-ELEVATIONS-SECTIONS-SCALE ¼ = 1'0"

NOTES
EXTERIOR WALLS BUILT OF RED BRICK
PLASTERED OUT AND INSIDE WITH
LIME AND CEMENT MORTAR 3" THICK.
FOUNDATION OF BLUE RUBBLE STONE.
LINTELS AND SILLS OF WHITE BEDFORD STONE.
TOP AND INTERIOR STAIRS, WINDOWS AND
DOORS BUILT OF WOOD.

KEY TO MATERIALS
RUBBLE BLUE NATIVE
WHITE BEDFORD CO
COMMON RED BR.
WOOD

GRAPHIC SCALES

U.S. DEPARTMENT OF THE INTERIOR
NATIONAL PARKS, BUILDINGS, AND RESERVATIONS
BRANCH OF PLANS AND DESIGN

| NAME OF STRUCTURE |
MINNESOTA POINT-LIGHT HOUSE - DULUTH MINN.

SURVEY NO.
29-23

HISTORIC AMERICAN
BUILDINGS SURVEY

(Above) These architectural drawings indicate the 40-foot tower's appearance at the time of its construction in 1858.

(Opposite page) Like a half-fallen industrial chimney from some long vanished factory, this ruined tower was once vital to Lake Superior's iron ore fleet. It is all that remains of the Minnesota Point Lighthouse near the entrance to Duluth Harbor. The light station was abandoned in 1878 after sand and silt plugged the nearby channel.

RUBICON POINT LIGHTHOUSE

Fort Bliss State Park, Lake Tahoe, California

1919

A lighthouse in the Sierra Nevadas? You bet! In 1919 the government established a modest navigational light on the southwestern shores of Lake Tahoe. The job assigned to this little lighthouse—not much taller than a person—was to guide the steamers carrying passengers, mail, and supplies to the small communities that dot the shores of this extraordinary high sierra lake.

Located atop lofty Rubicon Point at 6,300-foot elevation, it was unquestionably the highest lighthouse in America. Built on a budget of only about $760 for lumber, concrete, and other materials and with $40 for labor, it was also one of the cheapest. The keeper who looked after the light was paid $180 a year for his services. Fuel for the small lamp was supplied by 300-pound tanks of acetylene hauled to the site by mules.

Discontinued sometime during the 1930s, the tower still stands. Plans are being made to restore it for use as a historical attraction.

Lighthouse Digest

The Rubicon Point Lighthouse on Lake Tahoe. Visitors to Fort Bliss State Park have been known to mistake the structure for an outhouse.

HELP SAVE A LIGHTHOUSE

*Y*ou pick up the morning paper. "Washington Monument Demolished, Statue of Liberty to Follow!"the headline says. "How could this be?"you wonder. The story explains that for years a small group of dedicated people had been trying to the raise the money needed to restore these venerable structures, but since their efforts were unsuccessful, both monuments have deteriorated beyond repair and must be torn down.

You had heard about these efforts in the past but always thought, "What could possibly happen? These are historic landmarks. Surely the government would never allow them to be destroyed!" You had considered sending a donation, but just never had the time or the extra $10. Besides, what difference would your measly $10 have made anyway?

You may think this scenario sounds far-fetched—and probably nothing of the sort could ever happen to Washington's famed obelisk or to New York City's Lady Liberty. But it may surprise you to learn that dozens of stories very like the one above could be told about many of our other national treasures, and unfortunately those stories are all too true. As reminders of a maritime heritage we cannot afford to forget, our nation's historic lighthouses are important national monuments in their own right. Yet many of them have already been lost due to erosion, neglect, and vandalism. Many more are in danger of being lost.

While it is true that many of our nation's lighthouses have been saved and are now open to the public as museums, hostels, and bed-and-breakfasts, many others may soon be lost forever. These endangered lights are in desperate need of helping hands. Much has already been accomplished, but even more hard work remains to be done. In previous sections of this book, you've read about the highly publicized rescue of North Carolina's Cape Hatteras Lighthouse, the tallest light in America. You've learned how Cape Cod's historic Highland Light and Rhode Island's classic Southeast Light on Block Island were rolled back from the very edge of crumbling cliffs. There are many other success stories, such as the Great Lakes Lighthouse Keepers Association restoration of the remote St. Helena Lighthouse in Michigan and of the Round Island Lighthouse in the Straits of Mackinac. But for every such story with a happy ending there are ten or more orphaned lighthouses, some of them seriously threatened.

Throughout the country small volunteer groups are working day and night to raise the money needed to restore and save lighthouses. However, their time and funding are invariably limited. Who will help them when they have used up all their local resources?

One organization that has recently stepped forward to help is the American Lighthouse Foundation (ALF), a non-profit group of volunteers dedicated to saving America's lighthouses through national media attention, fund-raising, and actual restoration. Headquartered in Wells, Maine, the foundation has a nationwide membership. Its work is supported by small individual and corporate donations. The foundation assists smaller, local lighthouse preservation groups and has a number of lighthouses under its direct care. The foundation has also sponsored lighthouse events and conferences, supported initiatives across the United States and Canada, and promoted local and national lighthouse preservation through political contacts.

We urge you to get involved with a lighthouse group in your area to help save our nation's maritime heritage. If you do not live near a community with such a group, pick a favorite lighthouse and join the group working to restore that one. Or join the American Lighthouse Foundation and help its members preserve our nation's lighthouse history and heritage. You can make a difference.

Lighthouses helped save lives. It's our turn to save them.

Ruins of the Pelee Island Lighthouse in Ontario as it looked in 1999. Thanks to the dedicated efforts of local lighthouse preservationists, the tower has recently been fully restored.

FRIENDS OF THE LIGHTS

A LIST OF LIGHTHOUSE ORGANIZATIONS

To find out how you can help save America's endangered lighthouses, contact one or more of the following organizations:

American Lighthouse Foundation
Post Office Box 889
Wells, Maine 04090

Cape St. George Lighthouse
Save the Light
Post Office Box 915
Apalachicola, Florida 32329

Crisp Point Lighthouse
Crisp Point Lighthouse Historical Society
Post Office Box 229
Paradise, Michigan 49768

Dutch Island Lighthouse
Dutch Island Lighthouse Preservation Society
Chapter of American Lighthouse Foundation
Post Office Box 40151
Providence, Rhode Island 02940

Esopus Meadows Lighthouse
Save Esopus Lighthouse Commission
Post Office Box 1290
Port Ewen, New York 12466

Faulkner's Island Lighthouse
Faulkner's Island Light Brigade
Post Office Box 199
Guilford, Connecticut 06437

Huron Island Lighthouse
Huron Island Lighthouse Preservation Association
Post Office Box 381
L'Anse, Michigan 49946

Little River Lighthouse
American Lighthouse Foundation
Post Office Box 889
Wells, Maine 04090

Mohawk Island Lighthouse
Mohawk Lighthouse Preservation Association
RR 2, Lowbanks, Ontario NOA 1KO
Canada

Morris Island Lighthouse
Save the Lighthouse, Inc.
Post Office Box 12490
Charleston, South Carolina 29422

Nauset Beach Lighthouse
Nauset Light Preservation Society
Post Office Box 941
Eastham, Massachusetts 02642

Plum Beach Lighthouse
Friends of Plum Beach Lighthouse, Inc.
Post Office Box 451
Portsmouth, Rhode Island 02871

Sand Island Lighthouse
Sand Island Lighthouse Preservation Group, Inc.
6148 Old Pascagoula Road
Theodore, Alabama 36582

Sankaty Head Lighthouse
Sconset Trust
Post Office Box 821
Siasconset, Massachusetts 02564

South Fox Island Lighthouse
South Fox Island Project
Post Office Box 25
Interlochen, Michigan 49643
or
South Fox Lighthouse Association
2549 Otter
Warren, Michigan 48092

St. Helena Island Lighthouse
Great Lakes Lighthouse Keepers Association
Post Office Box 580
Allen Park, Michigan 48101

INDEX OF LIGHTHOUSES